PERIPHERAL DEVICE INTERFACES	
READING AND WRITING DATA WITH PER	
CLOCKING PERIPHERALS	101
ENABLING AND DISABLING PERIPHERAL DEVICES	104
HANDLING INTERRUPTS	106
PIN ALTERNATE FUNCTIONS	107

DEBUGGING GPIO — 108

EXAMPLE 1	109
EXAMPLE 2	113
EXAMPLE 3	118
EXAMPLE 4	121
EXAMPLE 5	126
EXAMPLE 6	131

DEBUGGING TIMERS — 133

CONFIGURING AND DEBUGGING PWM	134
BUILDING A LOGIC ANALYZER FOR TIMERS: EXAMPLE 1	140
BUILDING A LOGIC ANALYZER FOR TIMERS: EXAMPLE 2	143
BUILDING A LOGIC ANALYZER FOR TIMERS: EXAMPLE 3	145
TIMER INTERRUPT HANDLING: EXAMPLE 1	149
TIMER INTERRUPT HANDLING: EXAMPLE 2	152

DEBUGGING DIRECT DIGITAL SYNTHESIS APPLICATIONS — 153

BUILDING A LOGIC ANALYZER: EXAMPLE 1	153
BUILDING A LOGIC ANALYZER: EXAMPLE 2	157
BUILDING A LOGIC ANALYZER: EXAMPLE 3	158
BUILDING A LOGIC ANALYZER: EXAMPLE 4	163

MEASURING AND TRACING ANALOG SIGNALS — 164

EXAMPLE 1	165
EXAMPLE 2	171

INDEX — 174

Introduction

This book aims at those who want to learn ARM code debugging in the free popular STM32CubeIDE environment. The material of this book can be considered as a highly practical guide for the readers who have basic skills in programming embedded systems with ARM microcontrollers.
All applications described in this book were tested on the NUCLEO-L476RG development board, although they can easily be adapted to other development boards equipped with STM32 Cortex-M4/L4/M7 microcontrollers with the minor changes in software.
All source code from this book was developed using the STM32CubeIDE 1.5.0 development environment.

Disclaimer

While the author has used good faith efforts to ensure that the information and instructions contained in this book are accurate, the author disclaims all responsibility for errors or omissions, including without limitation responsibility for damages resulting from the use of or reliance on this work. Use of the information and instructions contained in this work is at your own risk. If any code samples or other technology this book contains or describes is subject to open source licenses or the intellectual property rights of others, it is your responsibility to ensure that your use thereof complies with such licenses and/or rights. All example applications from this book were developed and tested without damaging hardware. The author will not accept any responsibility for damages of any kind due to actions taken by you after reading this book.

Hardware and software

The material of this book is based upon using the free and easy to use STM32CubeIDE 1.5.0 development environment that provides great capabilities for both beginners and experienced developers.
To program and debug the demo applications from this book, the author used a popular low-cost NUCLEO-L476RG development board (**Fig.1**) that is described in detail on www.st.com.

Learn to Debug ARM code
With
STM32 Microcontrollers

A Practical Guide

By Yury Magda

Copyright © 2020 by Yury Magda. All rights reserved.

The programs, examples, and applications presented in this book have been included for their instructional value. The author offers no warranty implied or express, including but not limited to implied warranties of fitness or merchantability for any particular purpose and do not accept any liability for any loss or damage arising from the use of any information in this book, or any error or omission in such information, or any incorrect use of these programs, procedures, and applications.
No part of this publication may be reproduced, stored in a retrieval system, or transmitted in any form or by any means, electronic, mechanical, photocopying, recording, or otherwise, without the prior written permission of the author.

To my wife, Julia

About the Author

Yury Magda is an embedded engineer experienced in designing hardware and software for Intel x86- and ARM-based systems. He is also the author of the books on designing embedded systems based upon various development platforms.

Contents

INTRODUCTION	**6**
DISCLAIMER	**6**
HARDWARE AND SOFTWARE	**6**
DEBUGGING FOR BEGINNERS: PRELIMINARY STEPS	**7**
Step 1: Choosing demo code	7
Step 2: Modifying a basic STM32 code	8
Step 3: Configuring the Debugger	13
WATCHING DATA IN STM32CUBEIDE	**16**
ANALYZING DISASSEMBLY BY EXAMPLE	**23**
Adding data to watch	25
Using the Disassembly window	30
Breaking down disassembly	33
Analyzing Disassembly Fragments	37
OUTPUT DATA IN THE DEBUGGER	**57**
Using SWD interface	58
Using USB-UART interface	67
PROGRAMMABLE BREAKPOINTS	**75**
Example 1	76
Example 2	77
HANDLING EXCEPTIONS	**78**
Example 1	78
Example 2	82
Example 3	86
USING SUPERVISOR CALLS	**89**
Example 1	89
Example 2	93
UNDERSTANDING STM32 PERIPHERALS	**97**
Accessing peripheral devices	98

Fig.1

The big advantage of all STM32 Nucleo boards is that they don't require any separate probe as they integrate the ST-LINK/V2-1 debugger and programmer. These boards come with the STM32 comprehensive software HAL library together with various packaged software examples.

Debugging For Beginners: Preliminary Steps

Debugging program code may be a complex task for beginners. There may be various ways of learning how to debug embedded code. The following sequence may simplify your start.

Step 1: Choosing demo code

Generally, we can take almost any high-level C/C++ source code, build the executable and start a debugging session. The disadvantage of such approach is that if we misunderstand the algorithm, we will not understand the code / data flow while debugging an application.
Therefore, it would be much better to learn debugging with simple algorithm(s) that we clearly understand. In this case, debugging the executable will be much easier, because we can guess what should happen at some particular point of code.

A few simple algorithms implemented in C (**Listing 1** - **Listing 3**) can be used as the starting points.

The source code fragment from **Listing 1** allows to calculate the sum of integers from 0 to 9.

Listing 1.

```
int sum = 0;
. . . . . . .
for (int i = 0; i < 10; i++)
    sum += i;
. . . . . . .
```

The code fragment in **Listing 2** allows to convert all negative numbers in the integer array into positive values.

Listing 2.

```
int a1[5] = {2, -5, -11, 9, 3};
for (int i = 0; i < 5; i++)
   if (a[i1] < 0) a[i1] = -a[i1];
```

One more code fragment in **Listing 3** allows to calculate the sum of the elements of an integer array using the pointers.

Listing 3.

```
int a1[5] = {2, -5, -11, 9, 3};
int *pa1 = a1;
int sum = 0;

for (int i = 0; i < 5; i++)
   sum += *pa1++;
```

Many code fragments similar to those shown above can be used while debugging code.
Those code fragments can be inserted into the **main()** function of the STM32 project as is illustrated in the next section.

Step 2: Modifying a basic STM32 code

Let's create a new STM32 project by choosing
File → New→ STM32 Project (Fig.2).

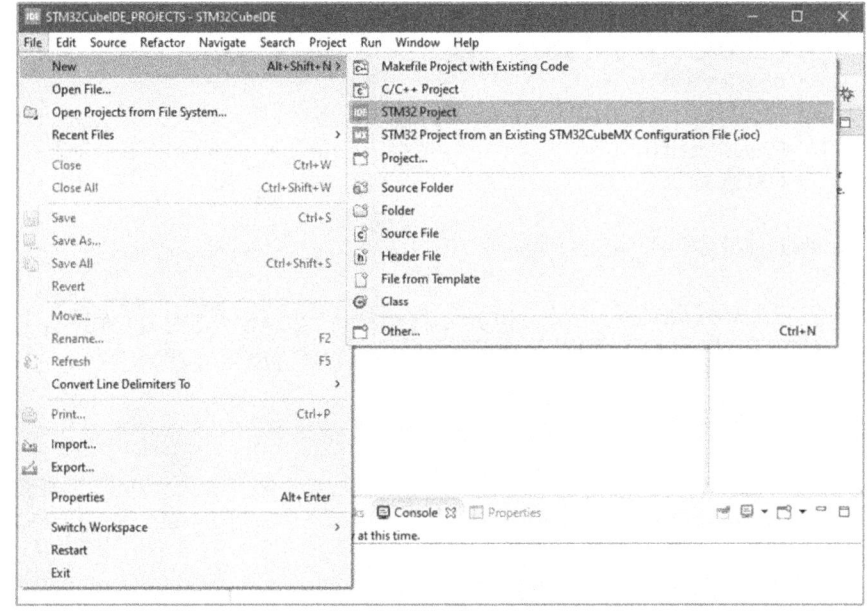

Fig.2

While creating the project, you may allow to initialize all peripheral devices with their default mode. When a Project Wizard finishes its job, we get a **main()** function with the source code generated according to the project settings (**Listing 4**). Further I will remove most comments in **main()** leaving only the code fragments of interest.

Listing 4.

#include "main.h"

/* Private includes --*/
/* USER CODE BEGIN Includes */

/* USER CODE END Includes */

/* Private typedef ---*/
/* USER CODE BEGIN PTD */

/* USER CODE END PTD */

/* Private define --*/
/* USER CODE BEGIN PD */
/* USER CODE END PD */

/* Private macro ---*/
/* USER CODE BEGIN PM */

/* USER CODE END PM */

/* Private variables ---*/
UART_HandleTypeDef huart2;

/* USER CODE BEGIN PV */

/* USER CODE END PV */

/* Private function prototypes ---*/
void SystemClock_Config(void);
static void MX_GPIO_Init(void);
static void MX_USART2_UART_Init(void);
/* USER CODE BEGIN PFP */

/* USER CODE END PFP */

/* Private user code ---*/
/* USER CODE BEGIN 0 */

/* USER CODE END 0 */

/**
  * @brief The application entry point.
  * @retval int
  */
int main(void)
{
  /* USER CODE BEGIN 1 */

```
/* USER CODE END 1 */

/* MCU Configuration--------------------------------------------------------*/

/* Reset of all peripherals, Initializes the Flash interface and the Systick. */
HAL_Init();

/* USER CODE BEGIN Init */

/* USER CODE END Init */

/* Configure the system clock */
SystemClock_Config();

/* USER CODE BEGIN SysInit */

/* USER CODE END SysInit */

/* Initialize all configured peripherals */
MX_GPIO_Init();
MX_USART2_UART_Init();
/* USER CODE BEGIN 2 */

/* USER CODE END 2 */

/* Infinite loop */
/* USER CODE BEGIN WHILE */
while (1)
{
  /* USER CODE END WHILE */

  /* USER CODE BEGIN 3 */
}
/* USER CODE END 3 */
}
. . . . . . .
```

Since I am going to debug some simple code fragment, I choose the following one (**Listing 5**) and insert it into the **main()** function.

Listing 5.

```
int sum = 0;
. . . . . . .
for (int i = 0; i < 10; i++)
   sum += i;
. . . . . . .
```

The above code calculates the sum of integers in the range of 0 to 9. The result will then be stored in the **sum** variable.
The modified **main()** source code will then look like the following (**Listing 6**).

Listing 6.

```
#include "main.h"
int sum = 0;
. . . . . . .

/* Private function prototypes ------------------------------------------*/
void SystemClock_Config(void);
static void MX_GPIO_Init(void);
static void MX_USART2_UART_Init(void);
. . . . . . .

int main(void)
{
  /* MCU Configuration-----------------------------------------------*/

  /* Reset of all peripherals, Initializes the Flash interface and the Systick. */
  HAL_Init();

  /* Configure the system clock */
  SystemClock_Config();

  /* Initialize all configured peripherals */
  MX_GPIO_Init();
  MX_USART2_UART_Init();
  /* USER CODE BEGIN 2 */
  . . . . . . .
```

```
for (int i1 = 0; i1 < 10; i1++)
    sum += i1;
. . . . . . .
while (1)
{
}
}
. . . . . .
```

After saving all changes, I will build the project. After my project is built without errors, I can examine the code by starting a debugging session.

Step 3: Configuring the Debugger

To start debugging code, we should simply click **Debug (Fig.3)**.

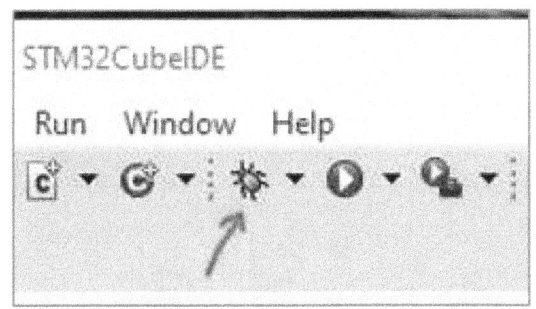

Fig.3

If a debugging session is started for the first time, the **Edit Configuration** window opens. Here we need to choose the **Debugger** option **(Fig.4)**.

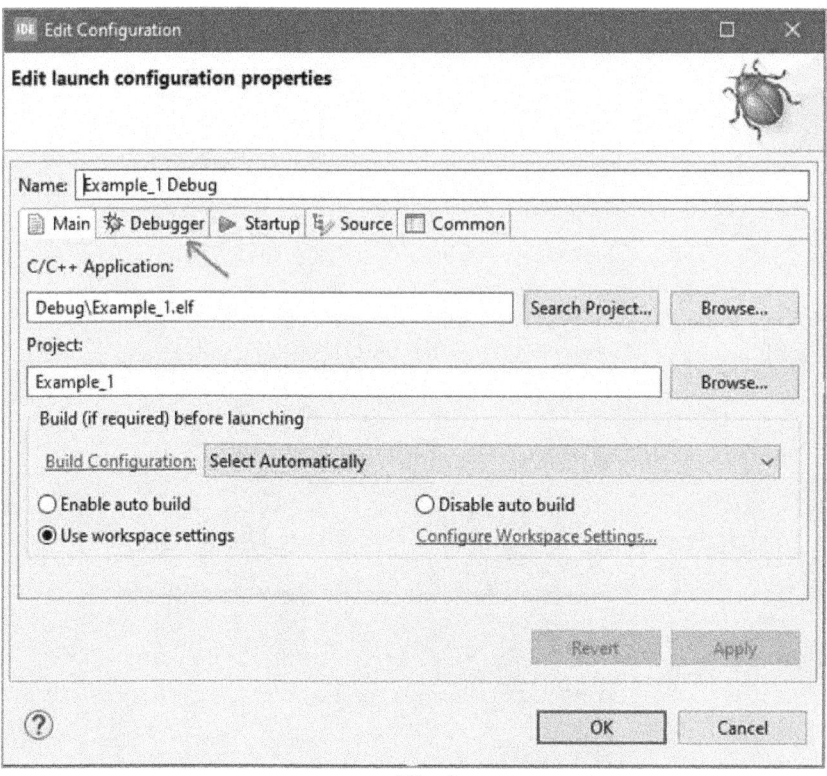

Fig.4

Setting the Debugger parameters depends on the type of the device we use. In my case, the NUCLEO-L476RG board has the integrated ST-LINK/V2-1 debugger and programmer, therefore the settings will look like the following (**Fig.5**).

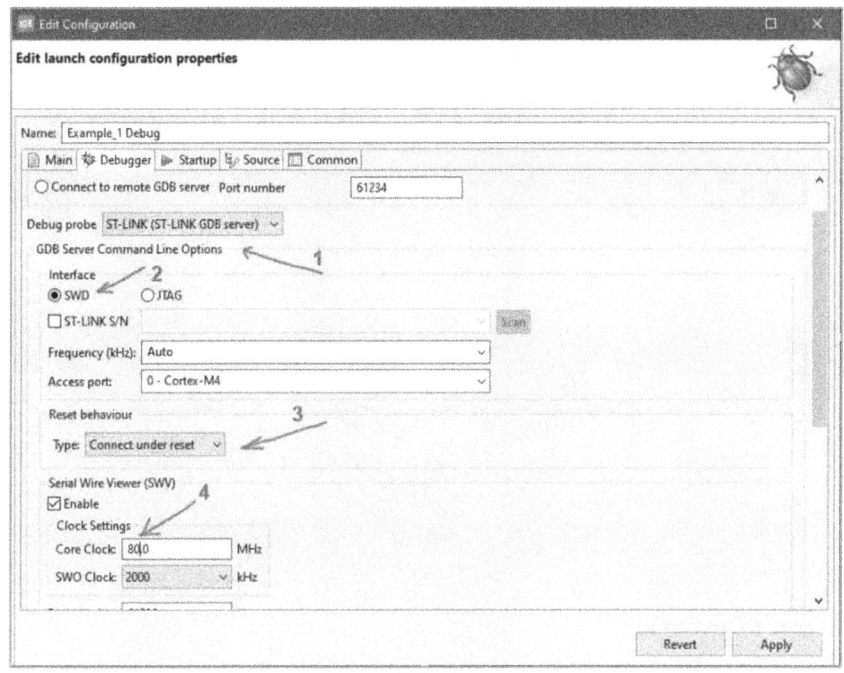

Fig.5

The **Debugger** parameters for the integrated debugger are detailed in the table below.

№	Parameter	Value
1	Debug probe	ST-LINK(ST-LINK GDB server)
2	Interface	SWD
3	Reset behavior (Type)	Connect under reset
4	Serial Wire Viewer (SWV)	Enable

When SWV is enabled, we need to set the **Core Clock** parameter. Its value can be retrieved from the **Clock Configuration** page of the project (**SYSCLK, Fig.6**). In my case, this value = 80 MHz.

15

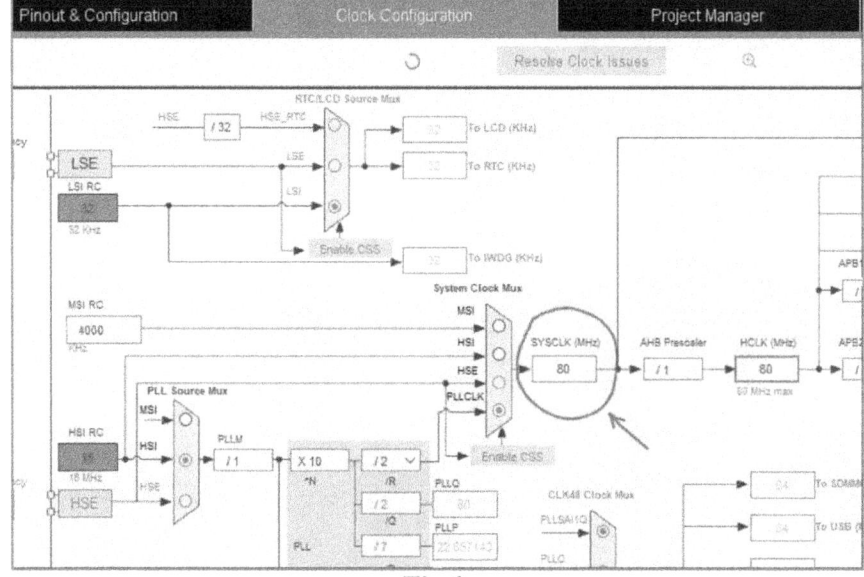

Fig.6

Clicking **Apply** completes configuring the **Debugger**.
Note that if you use a standalone ST-Link V2 adapter, you need to select **ST-LINK S/N** option, then scan the hardware to detect the serial number of the adapter by clicking **Scan** (see **Fig.5**).
These are the basic settings for the integrated ST-LINK debugger/programmer of my Nucleo board. If you use other device, for example, J-Link from Segger, the settings will be different.

Watching Data in STM32CubeIDE

In order to evaluate symbols and expressions while debugging, we can use either **Expressions** or **Live Expressions** window to display the item name, value, and type.
Assume we want to watch variables **i1** and **sum** from **Listing 6** in the **Live Expressions** window. After a debugging session is started, we can add both variables and their addresses to the **Live Expressions** window as is shown in **Fig.7**.

Expression	Type	Value
i1		Failed to evaluate expression
&i1		Failed to evaluate expression
(x)= sum	int	0
> ➔ &sum	int *	0x20000028 <sum>
✜ Add new expression		

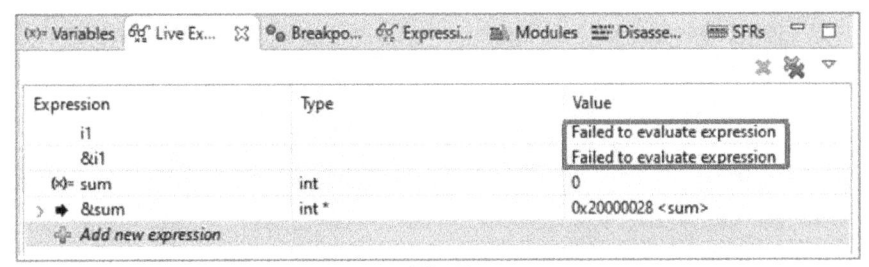

Fig.7

Note that when the debugging session is started, the initial value of variable **i1** is undefined because this variable will be initialized later in the **for()** loop. Therefore, we get the **"Failed to evaluate expression"** message after the Debugger has started. It is possible to avoid this message, if we define variable **i1** before the **for()** loop is entered (**Listing 7**).

Listing 7.

```
#include "main.h"
int i1;
int sum = 0;
. . . . . . .

for (i1 = 0; i1 < 10; i1++)
    sum += i1;
. . . . . . .
```

Once **i1** is defined, it is assigned 0 by default (**Fig.8**).

Expression	Type	Value
(x)= i1	int	0
> ➔ &i1	int *	0x200000ac <i1>
(x)= sum	int	0
> ➔ &sum	int *	0x20000028 <sum>
✜ Add new expression		

Fig.8

Then we can watch how variables **i1** and **sum** are updated within the **for()** loop. When the loop exits, **i1** and **sum** are assigned the following values (**Fig.9**).

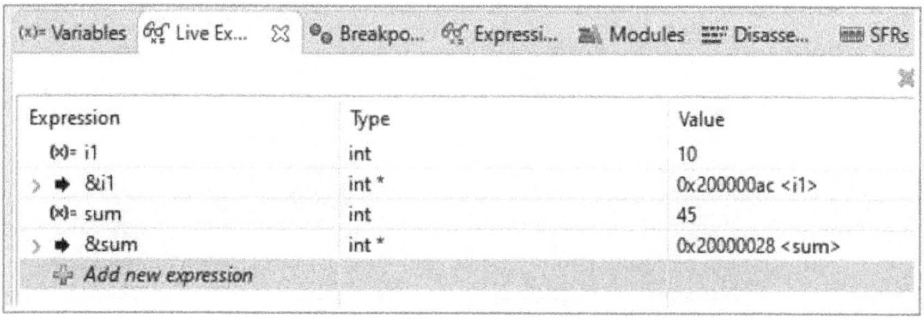

Expression	Type	Value
(x)= i1	int	10
> ➡ &i1	int *	0x200000ac <i1>
(x)= sum	int	45
> ➡ &sum	int *	0x20000028 <sum>
➕ Add new expression		

Fig.9

The **Expressions** and **Live Expressions** windows are handy when we trace the elements of arrays. For example, assume that we are debugging the code fragment shown in **Listing 8**.

Listing 8.

```
#include "main.h"
int a1[5] = {34, -7, 11, 3, -9};
int i1;
int sum = 0;
. . . . . . .
for (i1 = 0; i1 < sizeof(a1)/4; i1++)
{
  sum += a1[i1];
}
. . . . . . .
```

The above code calculates the sum of the elements of an integer array **a1**. To watch data while debugging, we can configure variables in the **Live Expressions** window as is shown in **Fig.10**.

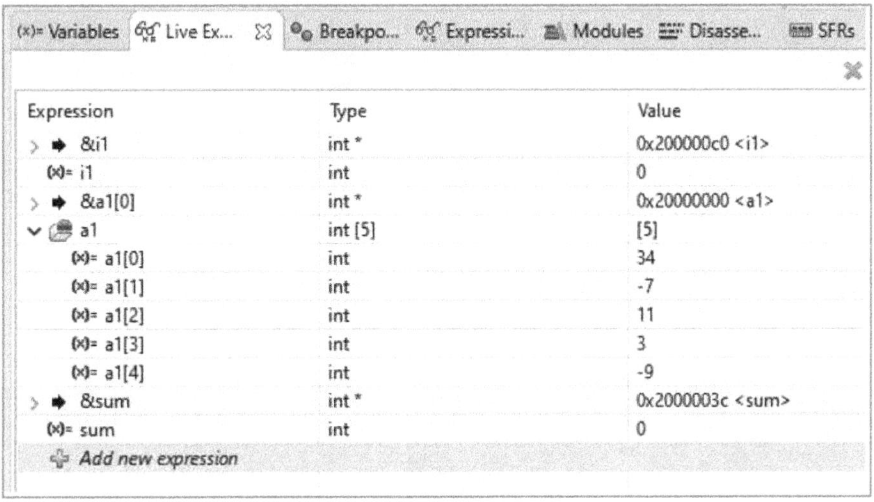

Expression	Type	Value
> ➔ &i1	int *	0x200000c0 <i1>
(x)= i1	int	0
> ➔ &a1[0]	int *	0x20000000 <a1>
˅ 🖻 a1	int [5]	[5]
(x)= a1[0]	int	34
(x)= a1[1]	int	-7
(x)= a1[2]	int	11
(x)= a1[3]	int	3
(x)= a1[4]	int	-9
> ➔ &sum	int *	0x2000003c <sum>
(x)= sum	int	0
➕ Add new expression		

Fig.10

Here we added array **a1** and its address that is **&a1[0]**.
Watching data gives us more useful information if we use pointers. Let's rewrite the code fragment calculating the sum of elements of an array so that to use pointers (**Listing 9**).

Listing 9.

```
#include "main.h"
int a1[5] = {34, -7, 11, 3, -9};
int *pa1 = a1;
int i1;
int sum = 0;
. . . . . . .
for (i1 = 0; i1 < sizeof(a1)/4; i1++)
{
  sum += *pa1++;
}
. . . . . . .
```

While debugging this code fragment, add the array **a1** and pointer **pa1** to the **Live Expression**s window. This allows to watch how both addresses and values are updated (**Fig.11**).

Expression	Type	Value
> ◆ &i1	int *	0x200000c4 <i1>
(x)= i1	int	1
∨ 🖼 a1	int [5]	[5]
(x)= a1[0]	int	34
(x)= a1[1]	int	-7
(x)= a1[2]	int	11
(x)= a1[3]	int	3
(x)= a1[4]	int	-9
∨ ◆ pa1	int *	0x20000008 <a1+8>
(x)= *pa1	int	11
> ◆ &sum	int *	0x20000040 <sum>
(x)= sum	int	27
➕ Add new expression		

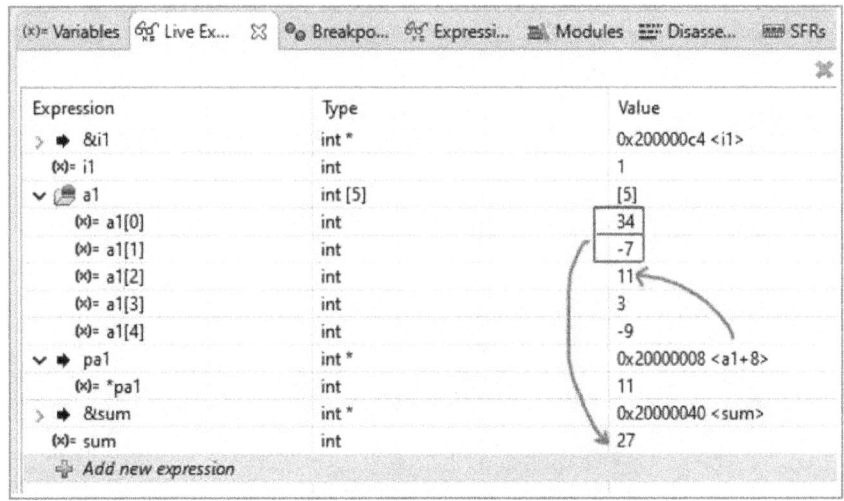

Fig.11

Specifically, **Fig.11** shows the state of variables after the second iteration (**i1** = 1). It is seen that **pa1** points to the element **a1[2]** stored at the address **a1+8**.

We can also watch data using the **Memory Browser** or **Memory** window. To use the **Memory Browser,** choose
Window → **Show View** → **Memory Browser** (**Fig.12**).

20

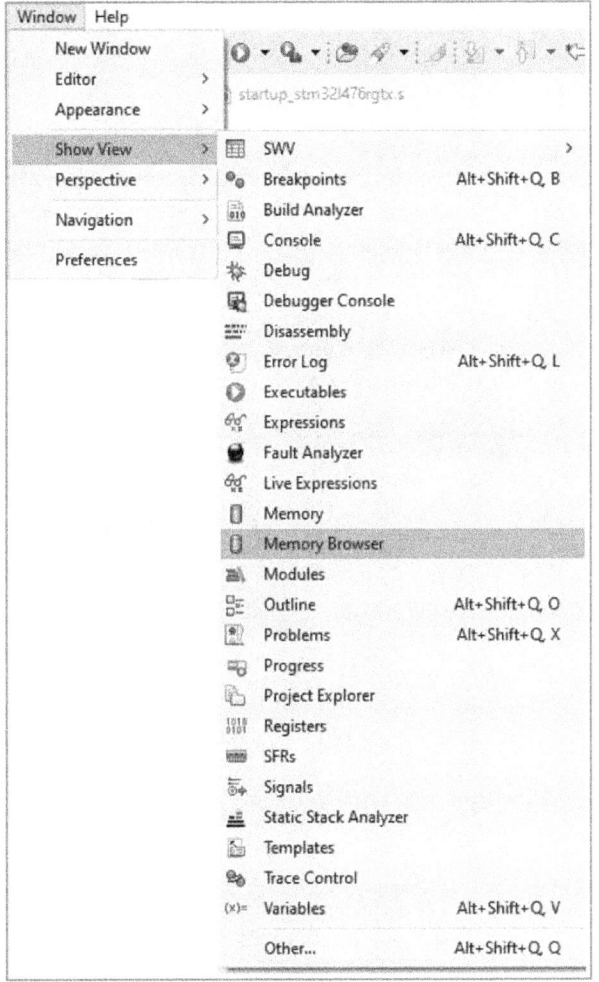

Fig.12

For example, after the second iteration has passed, the address and value of variable **sum** may look like the following (**Fig.13**).

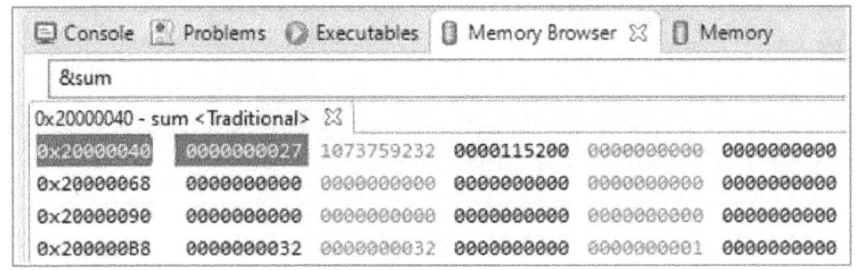

Fig.13

In order to use the **Memory** window, choose
Window → Show Window → Memory (Fig.14).

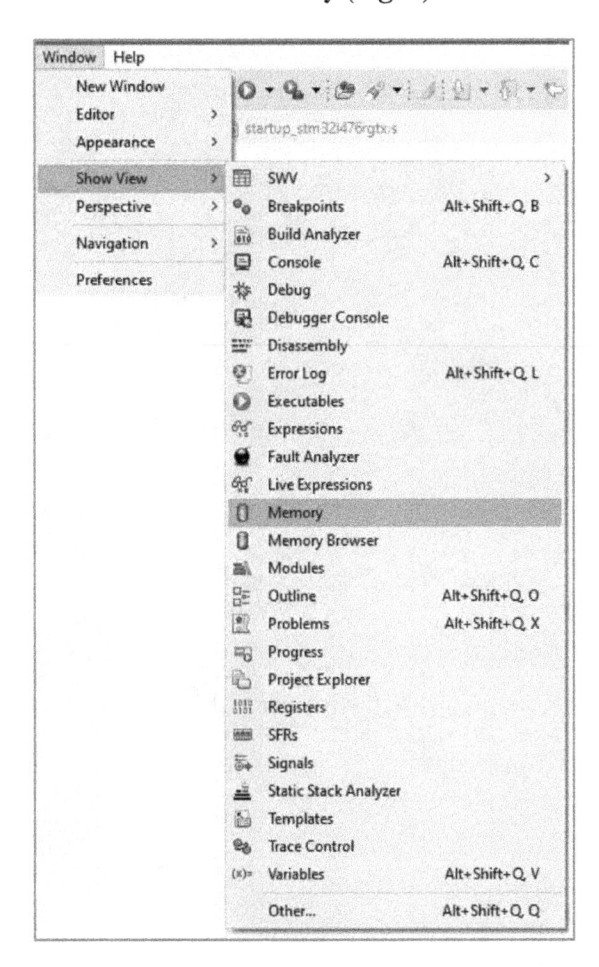

Fig.14

Then we can add variables to watch using the **Monitors** page as is illustrated in **Fig.15**.

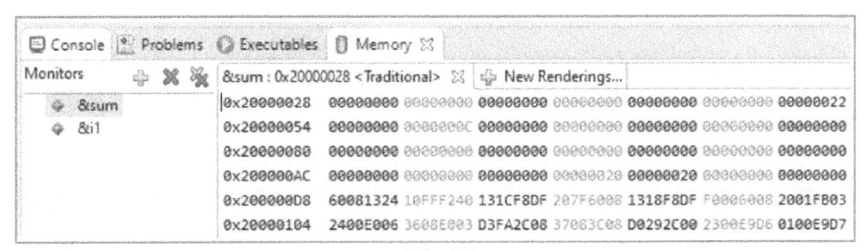

Fig.15

Here the **i1** and **sum** variables can be analyzed while debugging.

Analyzing Disassembly By Example

In this section, I will describe a simple practical approach to examine disassembly.
Let's take the following code fragment (**Listing 10**) for analyzing.

Listing 10.

```
int a1[5] = {12, -9, 5, 41, -5};
int *pa1 = a1;
int max;
. . . . . . .
max = *pa1++;
for (int i = 1; i < sizeof(a1)/4; i++)
{
if (max < *pa1) max = *pa1;
pa1++;
}
. . . . . . .
```

With this fragment, we can find the maximum element in the integer array **a1** and store this element in variable **max**.

Let's create a new STM32 project and insert the source code from **Listing 10** into the **main()** function. The modified **main()** function will then look like the following (**Listing 11**). The inserted lines are shown in bold.

Listing 11.

```
#include "main.h"
int a1[5] = {12, -9, 5, 41, -5};
int *pa1 = a1;
int max;

/* Private variables ---------------------------------------------------*/
UART_HandleTypeDef huart2;

/* Private function prototypes -----------------------------------------*/
void SystemClock_Config(void);
static void MX_GPIO_Init(void);
static void MX_USART2_UART_Init(void);

int main(void)
{
  /* Reset of all peripherals, Initializes the Flash interface and the Systick. */
  HAL_Init();

  /* Configure the system clock */
  SystemClock_Config();

  /* Initialize all configured peripherals */
  MX_GPIO_Init();
  MX_USART2_UART_Init();
  . . . . . . .

  max = *pa1++;
  for (int i = 1; i < sizeof(a1)/4; i++)
  {
    if (max < *pa1) max = *pa1;
    pa1++;
  }
```

```
  while (1)
  {
  }
}
. . . . . . .
```

Save changes and build the project. If there were no errors, we can start a debugging session.

Adding data to watch

While debugging, we usually need a few windows to watch data. One of them is a **Registers** window that allows to evaluate the core registers. This window will be opened by clicking **Window→ Show View→ Registers** (**Fig.16**).

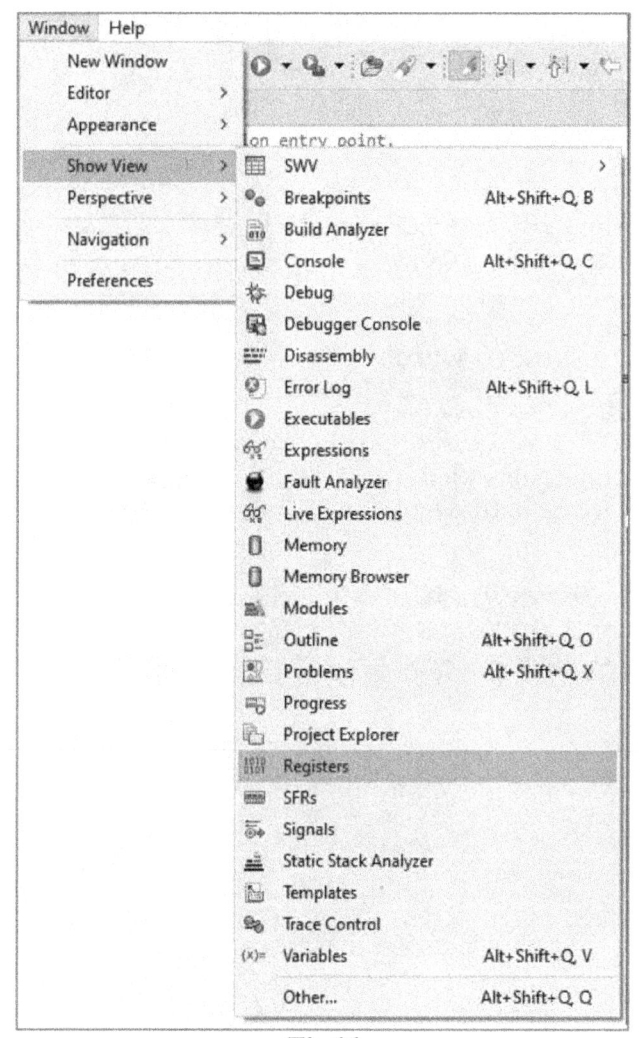

Fig.16

Also, we need the **Expressions** window (**Fig.17**) that will be opened by clicking **Window** → **Show View** → **Expressions**.

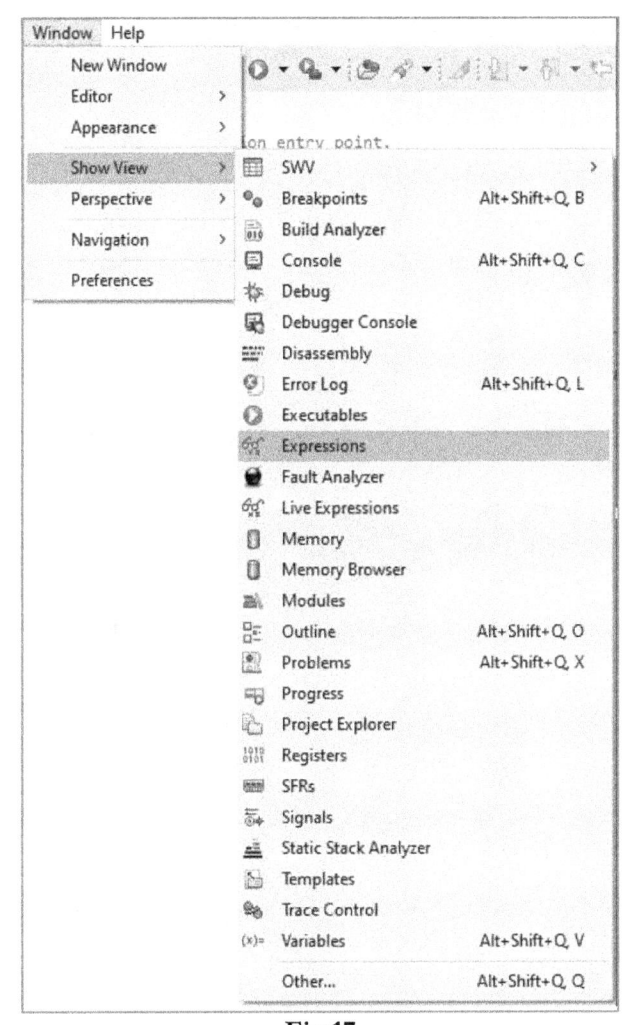

Fig.17

In this window, we will add the variables to watch by clicking "**+**"as is illustrated for variable **a1** (**Fig.18** - **Fig.19**).

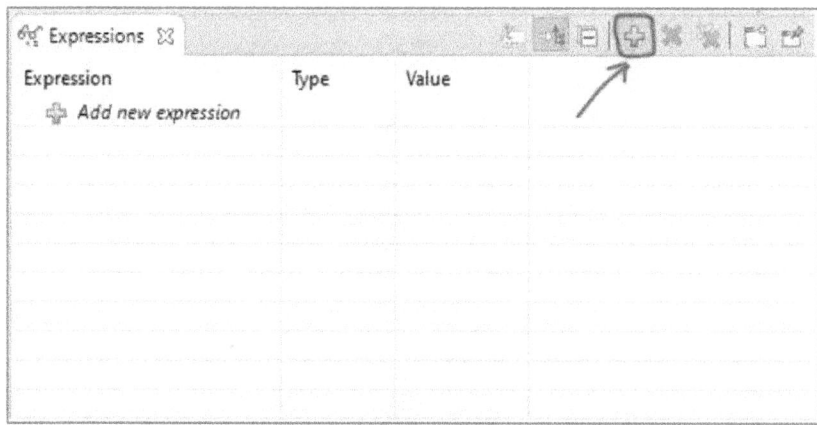

Fig.18

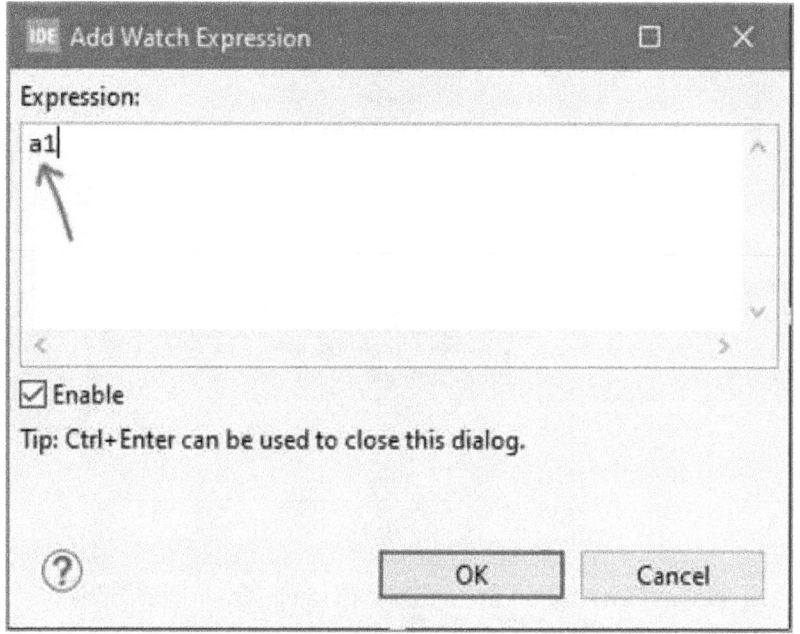

Fig.19

When we are done, the **Expressions** window will look like the following (**Fig.20**).

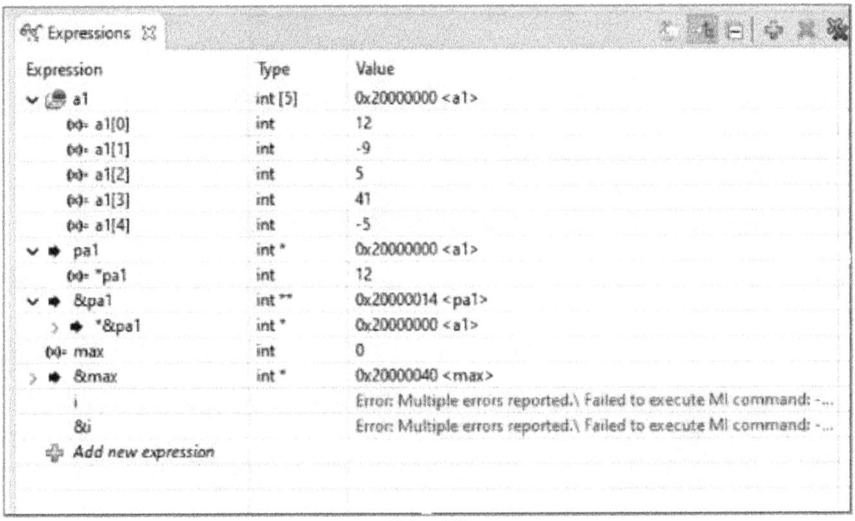

Expression	Type	Value
⌄ 🖳 a1	int [5]	0x20000000 <a1>
◦= a1[0]	int	12
◦= a1[1]	int	-9
◦= a1[2]	int	5
◦= a1[3]	int	41
◦= a1[4]	int	-5
⌄ ◆ pa1	int *	0x20000000 <a1>
◦= *pa1	int	12
⌄ ◆ &pa1	int **	0x20000014 <pa1>
⟩ ◆ *&pa1	int *	0x20000000 <a1>
◦= max	int	0
⟩ ◆ &max	int *	0x20000040 <max>
i		Error: Multiple errors reported.\ Failed to execute MI command: -...
&i		Error: Multiple errors reported.\ Failed to execute MI command: -...
⊕ Add new expression		

Fig.20

The next diagram (**Fig.21**) clarifies what is shown in the **Expressions** window.

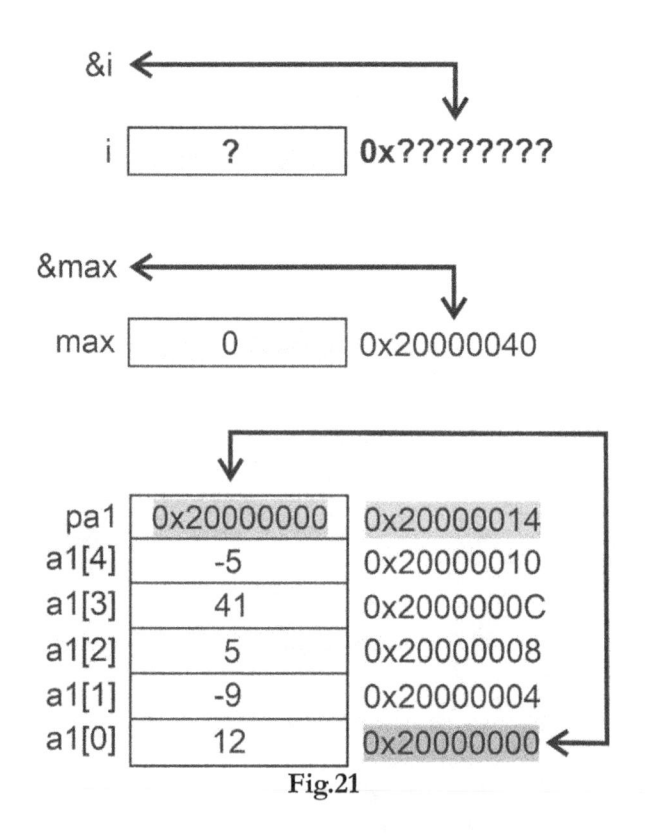

```
        &i ←─────────────┐
                         ↓
         i  [    ?    ]  0x????????


       &max ←─────────────┐
                          ↓
        max [    0    ]  0x20000040


                    ┌─────────────────┐
                    ↓                 │
        pa1 [ 0x20000000 ]  0x20000014
       a1[4] [    -5    ]  0x20000010
       a1[3] [    41    ]  0x2000000C
       a1[2] [     5    ]  0x20000008
       a1[1] [    -9    ]  0x20000004
       a1[0] [    12    ]  0x20000000 ←┘
                  Fig.21
```

Note that all variables are assigned their initial values when the debugging session is started.

Using the Disassembly window

Disassembly allows us to understand how code runs at the level of microcontroller (MCU) instructions. To view disassembly, we first need to open the **Disassembly** window. This window shows the program execution in assembly code that is intermixed with the source code.
To open the **Disassembly** window, click
Window → Show View → Disassembly (Fig.22).

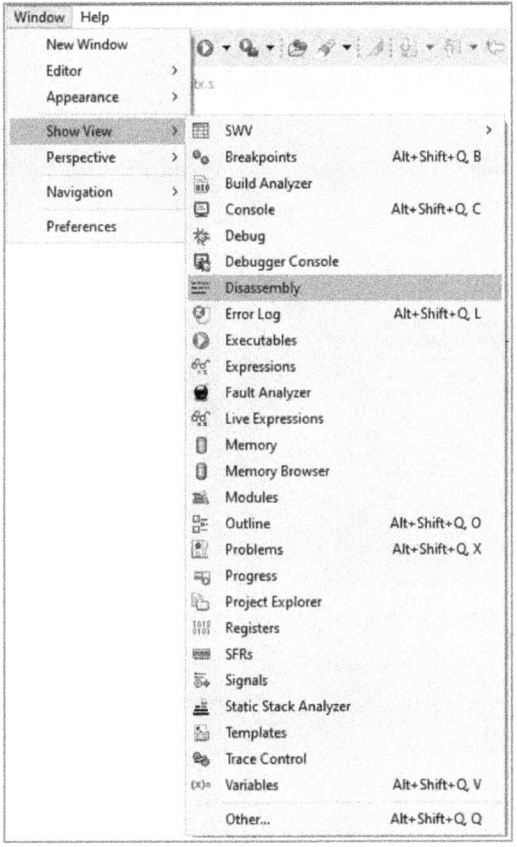

Fig.22

In our case, the **Disassembly** window will look like the following (**Fig.23**).

```
Disassembly ☒                              Enter location here

                            main:
080004c9:  main+0             push    {r7, lr}
080004cb:  main+2             sub     sp, #8
080004cd:  main+4             add     r7, sp, #0
     78                       HAL_Init();
✦ 080004ce:  main+6           bl      0x8000940 <HAL_Init>
     85                       SystemClock_Config();
080004d2:  main+10            bl      0x800052c <SystemClock_Config>
     92                       MX_GPIO_Init();
080004d6:  main+14            bl      0x8000678 <MX_GPIO_Init>
     93                       MX_USART2_UART_Init();
080004da:  main+18            bl      0x8000618 <MX_USART2_UART_Init>
    100                       max = *pa1++;
080004de:  main+22            ldr     r3, [pc, #68]   ; (0x8000524 <main+92>)
080004e0:  main+24            ldr     r3, [r3, #0]
080004e2:  main+26            adds    r2, r3, #4
080004e4:  main+28            ldr     r1, [pc, #60]   ; (0x8000524 <main+92>)
080004e6:  main+30            str     r2, [r1, #0]
080004e8:  main+32            ldr     r3, [r3, #0]
080004ea:  main+34            ldr     r2, [pc, #60]   ; (0x8000528 <main+96>)
080004ec:  main+36            str     r3, [r2, #0]
    101                       for (int i = 1; i < sizeof(a1)/4; i++)
080004ee:  main+38            movs    r3, #1
080004f0:  main+40            str     r3, [r7, #4]
080004f2:  main+42            b.n     0x800051c <main+84>
    103                       if (max < *pa1) max = *pa1;
080004f4:  main+44            ldr     r3, [pc, #44]   ; (0x8000524 <main+92>)
080004f6:  main+46            ldr     r3, [r3, #0]
080004f8:  main+48            ldr     r2, [r3, #0]
080004fa:  main+50            ldr     r3, [pc, #44]   ; (0x8000528 <main+96>)
080004fc:  main+52            ldr     r3, [r3, #0]
080004fe:  main+54            cmp     r2, r3
08000500:  main+56            ble.n   0x800050c <main+68>
08000502:  main+58            ldr     r3, [pc, #32]   ; (0x8000524 <main+92>)
08000504:  main+60            ldr     r3, [r3, #0]
08000506:  main+62            ldr     r3, [r3, #0]
08000508:  main+64            ldr     r2, [pc, #28]   ; (0x8000528 <main+96>)
0800050a:  main+66            str     r3, [r2, #0]
    104                       pa1++;
0800050c:  main+68            ldr     r3, [pc, #20]   ; (0x8000524 <main+92>)
0800050e:  main+70            ldr     r3, [r3, #0]
08000510:  main+72            adds    r3, #4
08000512:  main+74            ldr     r2, [pc, #16]   ; (0x8000524 <main+92>)
08000514:  main+76            str     r3, [r2, #0]
    101                       for (int i = 1; i < sizeof(a1)/4; i++)
08000516:  main+78            ldr     r3, [r7, #4]
08000518:  main+80            adds    r3, #1
```

Fig.23

It would be convenient to display the function offsets (outlined in **Fig.23**). To set this option, right-click in the disassembly window and check the corresponding option as is illustrated in **Fig.24**.

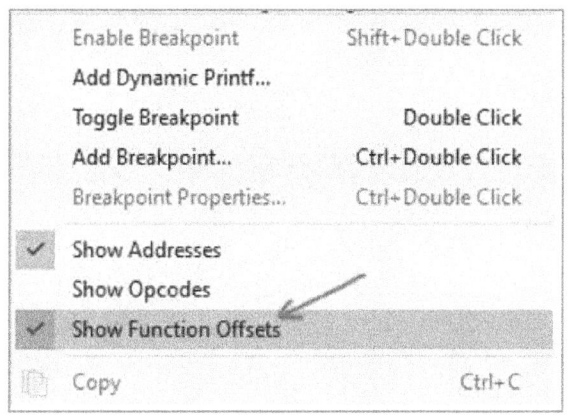

Fig.24

While analyzing disassembly, it would be nice to arrange the source code (1), **Registers** (2), **Expressions** (3) and **Disassembly** (4) windows so that to easily observe both code and data as is illustrated in **Fig.25**.

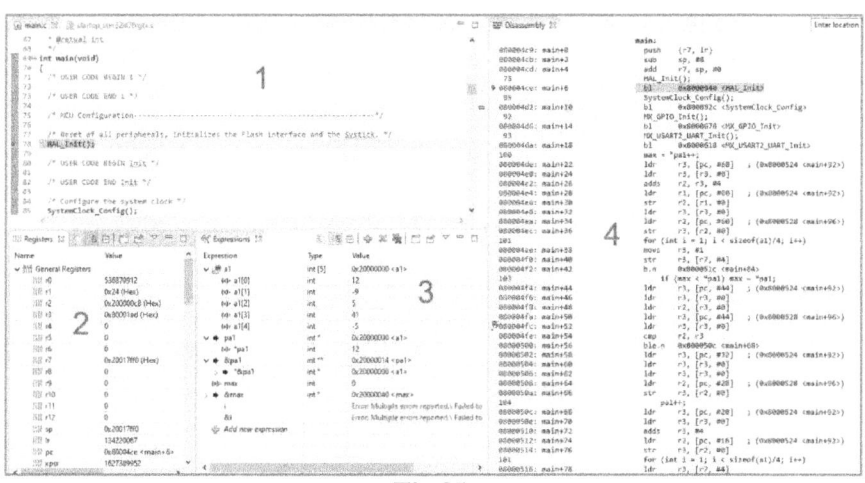

Fig.25

Breaking down disassembly

Analyzing even the small disassembly may be difficult enough, therefore it would be wise to break down disassembly into the relatively independent fragments (sections) - this can essentially simplify further analysis.

The disassembly of code that we want to analyze begins with the statement

max = *pa1++;

followed by the low-level code sequence shown in **Listing 12**.

Listing 12.

```
                        max = *pa1++;
080004de: main+22    ldr    r3, [pc, #68]  ; (0x8000524 <main+92>)
080004e0: main+24    ldr    r3, [r3, #0]
080004e2: main+26    adds   r2, r3, #4
080004e4: main+28    ldr    r1, [pc, #60]  ; (0x8000524 <main+92>)
080004e6: main+30    str    r2, [r1, #0]
080004e8: main+32    ldr    r3, [r3, #0]
080004ea: main+34    ldr    r2, [pc, #60]  ; (0x8000528 <main+96>)
080004ec: main+36    str    r3, [r2, #0]
```

It is seen that the above code fragment is linear, without branching, that simplifies analyzing. For convenience, we name the above code fragment **Fragment 1**.

The next statement shown in the **Disassembly** window is **for()**:

for (int i = 1; i < sizeof(a1)/4; i++)

Usually, such high-level logical structure is broken down into a few low-level code fragments scattered over disassembly. To determine all code fragments belonging to the **for()** logical statement, we should search the pairs of MCU instructions like the following

cmp
bl   <label>

In this particular case, searching through the **Disassembly** window gives us the bunch of MCU instructions (**Listing 13**) that assumingly make up the **for()** loop.

Listing 13.

```
                        for (int i = 1; i < sizeof(a1)/4; i++)
080004ee: main+38       movs    r3, #1
080004f0: main+40       str     r3, [r7, #4]
080004f2: main+42       b.n     0x800051c <main+84>

. . . . . . . . . .
080004f4: main+44       <other code>
. . . . . . .

                        for (int i = 1; i < sizeof(a1)/4; i++)
08000516: main+78       ldr     r3, [r7, #4]
08000518: main+80       adds    r3, #1
0800051a: main+82       str     r3, [r7, #4]
0800051c: main+84       ldr     r3, [r7, #4]
0800051e: main+86       cmp     r3, #4
08000520: main+88       bls.n   0x80004f4 <main+44>
. . . . . . .
```

It is seen that the above bunch of instructions includes two code fragments scattered over the **Disassembly** window. I named these code fragments **Fragment 2 and Fragment 5**.

One more statement to consider is

if (max < *pa1) max = *pa1;

The **if ()** logical structure is broken down into the following sequence of MCU instructions (**Listing 14**).

Listing 14.

```
. . . . . .
                        if (max < *pa1) max = *pa1;
080004f4: main+44       ldr     r3, [pc, #44]   ; (0x8000524 <main+92>)
080004f6: main+46       ldr     r3, [r3, #0]
080004f8: main+48       ldr     r2, [r3, #0]
080004fa: main+50       ldr     r3, [pc, #44]   ; (0x8000528 <main+96>)
080004fc: main+52       ldr     r3, [r3, #0]
080004fe: main+54       cmp     r2, r3
08000500: main+56       ble.n   0x800050c <main+68>
```

```
08000502: main+58    ldr    r3, [pc, #32]   ; (0x8000524 <main+92>)
08000504: main+60    ldr    r3, [r3, #0]
08000506: main+62    ldr    r3, [r3, #0]
08000508: main+64    ldr    r2, [pc, #28]   ; (0x8000528 <main+96>)
0800050a: main+66    str    r3, [r2, #0]
. . . . . . .
```

I named the above sequence **Fragment 3**. The last high-level statement to consider is

pa1++;

Obviously, the above statement simply advances the pointer **pa1** to the next element in array **a1**. This statement is broken down into the following low-level sequence (**Listing 15**).

Listing 15.

```
. . . . . . .
                     pa1++;
0800050c: main+68    ldr    r3, [pc, #20]   ; (0x8000524 <main+92>)
0800050e: main+70    ldr    r3, [r3, #0]
08000510: main+72    adds   r3, #4
08000512: main+74    ldr    r2, [pc, #16]   ; (0x8000524 <main+92>)
08000514: main+76    str    r3, [r2, #0]
. . . . . . .
```

I named this sequence **Fragment 4**.
Finally, there will be 5 fragments of disassembly that we are going to examine separately from each other (**Fig.26**). Each fragment can be reached by executing a single-step into / over a function (instruction).

```
100                             max = *pa1++;
080004de: main+22               ldr    r3, [pc, #68]    ; (0x8000524 <main+92>)
080004e0: main+24               ldr    r3, [r3, #0]
080004e2: main+26               adds   r2, r3, #4
080004e4: main+28               ldr    r1, [pc, #60]    ; (0x8000524 <main+92>)
080004e6: main+30               str    r2, [r1, #0]     Fragment 1
080004e8: main+32               ldr    r3, [r3, #0]
080004ea: main+34               ldr    r2, [pc, #60]    ; (0x8000528 <main+96>)
080004ec: main+36               str    r3, [r2, #0]
101                             for (int i = 1; i < sizeof(a1)/4; i++)
080004ee: main+38               movs   r3, #1
080004f0: main+40               str    r3, [r7, #4]     Fragment 2
080004f2: main+42               b.n    0x800051c <main+84>
103                             if (max < *pa1) max = *pa1;
080004f4: main+44               ldr    r3, [pc, #44]    ; (0x8000524 <main+92>)
080004f6: main+46               ldr    r3, [r3, #0]
080004f8: main+48               ldr    r2, [r3, #0]
080004fa: main+50               ldr    r3, [pc, #44]    ; (0x8000528 <main+96>)
080004fc: main+52               ldr    r3, [r3, #0]
080004fe: main+54               cmp    r2, r3           Fragment 3
08000500: main+56               ble.n  0x800050c <main+68>
08000502: main+58               ldr    r3, [pc, #32]    ; (0x8000524 <main+92>)
08000504: main+60               ldr    r3, [r3, #0]
08000506: main+62               ldr    r3, [r3, #0]
08000508: main+64               ldr    r2, [pc, #28]    ; (0x8000528 <main+96>)
0800050a: main+66               str    r3, [r2, #0]
104                             pa1++;
0800050c: main+68               ldr    r3, [pc, #20]    ; (0x8000524 <main+92>)
0800050e: main+70               ldr    r3, [r3, #0]
08000510: main+72               adds   r3, #4           Fragment 4
08000512: main+74               ldr    r2, [pc, #16]    ; (0x8000524 <main+92>)
08000514: main+76               str    r3, [r2, #0]
101                             for (int i = 1; i < sizeof(a1)/4; i++)
08000516: main+78               ldr    r3, [r7, #4]
08000518: main+80               adds   r3, #1
0800051a: main+82               str    r3, [r7, #4]     Fragment 5
0800051c: main+84               ldr    r3, [r7, #4]
0800051e: main+86               cmp    r3, #4
08000520: main+88               bls.n  0x80004f4 <main+44>
```

Fig.26

Analyzing Disassembly Fragments

Fragment 1 (**Fig.27**) of disassembly corresponds to the statement

max = *pa1++; (1)

```
100    max = *pa1++;
101    for (int i = 1; i < sizeof(a1)/4; i++)
102    {
103        if (max < *pa1) max = *pa1;
104        pa1++;
105    }
```

Fig.27

In the **Disassembly** window, the low-level code fragment corresponding to the statement (1) is shown in **Listing 16**.

Listing 16.

                      max = *pa1++;

080004de: main+22	ldr	r3, [pc, #68]	(0x8000524 <main+92>)
080004e0: main+24	ldr	r3, [r3, #0]	
080004e2: main+26	adds	r2, r3, #4	
080004e4: main+28	ldr	r1, [pc, #60]	(0x8000524 <main+92>)
080004e6: main+30	str	r2, [r1, #0]	
080004e8: main+32	ldr	r3, [r3, #0]	
080004ea: main+34	ldr	r2, [pc, #60]	(0x8000528 <main+96>)
080004ec: main+36	str	r3, [r2, #0]	

It is seen that the above code mainly contains **ldr** / **str** MCU instructions that usually implement the assignment operators in C.

Since the ARM microcontrollers can't directly process data located somewhere in memory, the pairs of MCU instructions such as

ldr r_x, [r_y, #offset]
str r_x, [r_y, #offset]

are only used to load (**ldr**) / store (**str**) data to / from memory.

All operations with data (addition, subtraction, comparison, etc.) in ARM processors are implemented using only the MCU core registers.

Let's back to **Listing 16**. Clicking either **Step Into** or **Step Over** brings us to the instruction

080004de: main+22   ldr   r3, [pc, #68]

Obviously, this instruction loads some data from memory into the core register **r3**. I don't know what is placed at the address

[pc, #68]

Also, I don't want to spend time by tracing the above address, therefore I will simply execute the **ldr** instruction and see what value will be stored in register **r3**.

After executing the instruction, it turns out that the register **r3** holds the address of memory where the pointer **pa1** resides (indicated by an arrow in the **Registers** window, **Fig.28**).

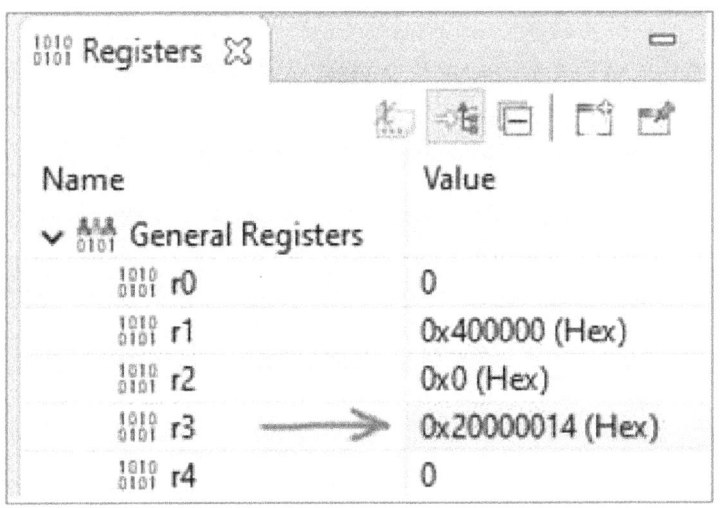

Name	Value
∨ General Registers	
r0	0
r1	0x400000 (Hex)
r2	0x0 (Hex)
r3	→ 0x20000014 (Hex)
r4	0

Fig.28

Examining the next instruction

080004e0: main+24   ldr   r3, [r3, #0]

hints me that the address of the array **a1** will move to register **r3**. Indeed, after executing this instruction, **r3** contains the address (=0x20000000) of the first element of array **a1**.

It is easily to notice that the sequence of two **ldr** instructions, wherever it appears, loads some value from memory to a core register.
The next instruction

080004e2: main+26   adds   r2, r3, #4

moves the value 0x20000004 into the register **r2** (indicated by an arrow in the **Registers** window, **Fig.29**).

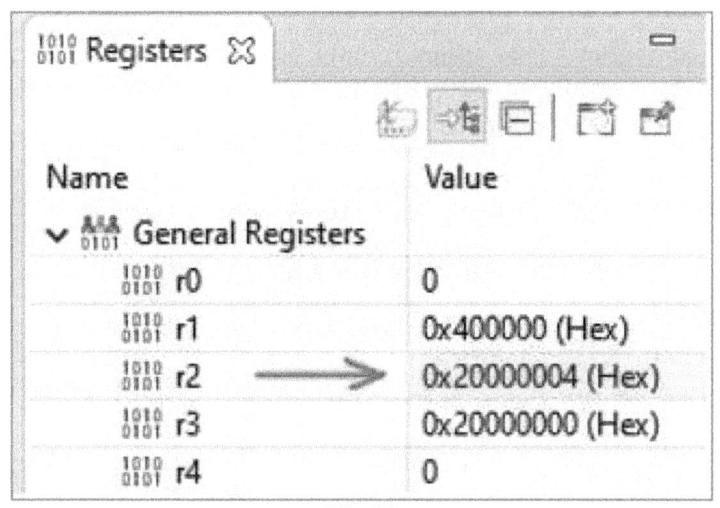

Name	Value
∨ General Registers	
r0	0
r1	0x400000 (Hex)
r2 ⟶	0x20000004 (Hex)
r3	0x20000000 (Hex)
r4	0

Fig.29

This value (=0x20000004) is the address of the element **a1[1]** of the array **a1**.
The next instruction

080004e4: main+28   ldr   r1, [pc, #60]

tells me that some value from the address

[pc, #60]

will be loaded into the core register **r1**. And again, at this point I don't have any idea what value will be stored in **r1** - it will be clear after the instruction has been executed.

After register **r1** is updated (indicated by an arrow in the **Registers** window, **Fig.30**), we will see that its value (=0x20000014) is the memory address where the pointer **pa1** is placed.

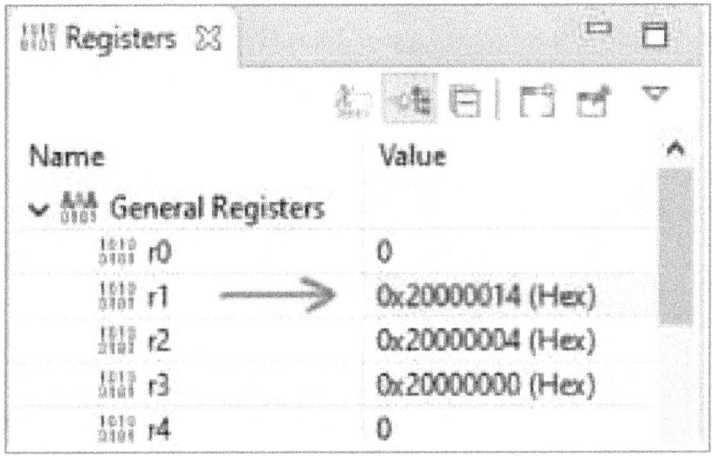

Fig.30

Name	Value
General Registers	
r0	0
r1	0x20000014 (Hex)
r2	0x20000004 (Hex)
r3	0x20000000 (Hex)
r4	0

Examining the next instruction

str r2, [r1, #0]

in the **Disassembly** window allows me to predict that the updated value of the pointer **pa1** placed in register **r2** will be stored at the memory address 0x20000014 placed in **r1**.
Clicking **Step Into** proves this. The updated values of **pa1** and **&pa1** are shown in the **Expressions** window (**Fig.31**).

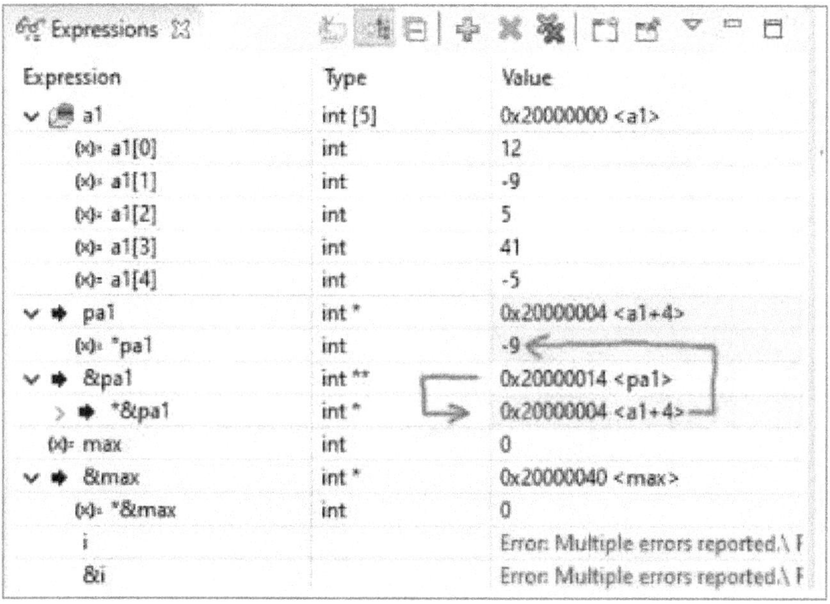

Expression	Type	Value
∨ a1	int [5]	0x20000000 <a1>
(x)= a1[0]	int	12
(x)= a1[1]	int	-9
(x)= a1[2]	int	5
(x)= a1[3]	int	41
(x)= a1[4]	int	-5
∨ pa1	int *	0x20000004 <a1+4>
(x)= *pa1	int	-9
∨ &pa1	int **	0x20000014 <pa1>
> *&pa1	int *	0x20000004 <a1+4>
(x)= max	int	0
∨ &max	int *	0x20000040 <max>
(x)= *&max	int	0
i		Error: Multiple errors reported.\ F
&i		Error: Multiple errors reported.\ F

Fig.31

Let's pause for a moment and summarize what has done. The sequence of instructions from the **Disassembly** window (**Listing 17**) simply advances the pointer **pa1** to the next element of the array **a1**.

Listing 17.

```
080004de: main+22    ldr    r3, [pc, #68]   (0x8000524 <main+92>)
080004e0: main+24    ldr    r3, [r3, #0]
080004e2: main+26    adds   r2, r3, #4
080004e4: main+28    ldr    r1, [pc, #60]   (0x8000524 <main+92>)
080004e6: main+30    str    r2, [r1, #0]
```

This sequence implements the high-level operation of incrementing the pointer **pa1**:

pa1++;

At this moment, the pointer **pa1** is advanced to the address of the element **a1[1]** of array **a1**.

It seems reasonable to assume that the following MCU instructions should assign the value of element **a1[0]** to the variable **max**. Let's examine the next instruction:

080004e8: main+32   ldr   r3, [r3, #0]

Before executing the **ldr** instruction, register **r3** contains the address of the first element **a1[0]**. After **ldr** is executed, **r3** will hold 0xc (=12) that is the value of **a1[0]**.
The instruction

080004ea: main+34   ldr   r2, [pc, #60]

loads the address of the variable **max** (=0x20000040) into register **r2** (indicated by an arrow in the **Registers** window, **Fig.32**).

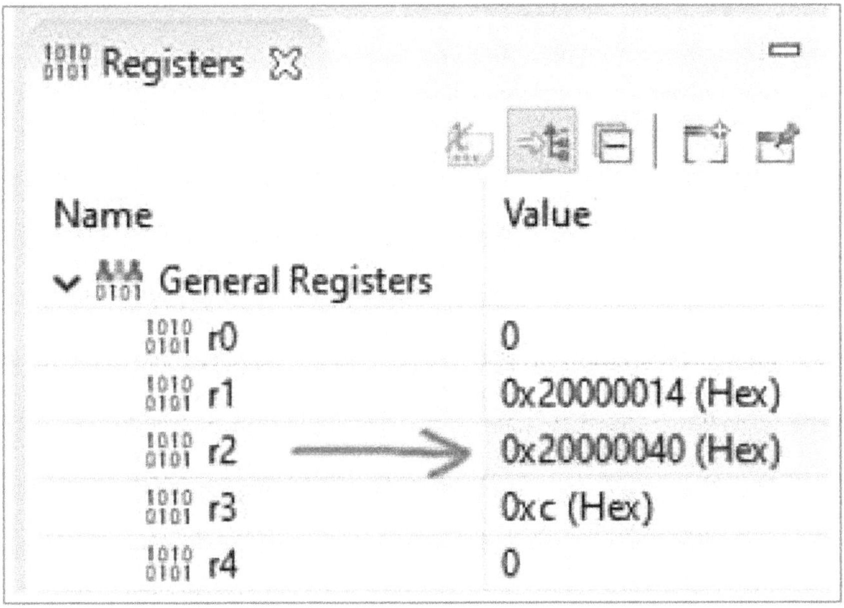

Name	Value
▾ General Registers	
r0	0
r1	0x20000014 (Hex)
r2 ⟶	0x20000040 (Hex)
r3	0xc (Hex)
r4	0

Fig.32

It is easily to understand that the next instruction

080004ec: main+36   str   r3, [r2, #0]

writes the value of **a1[0]** stored in register **r3** to the address of variable **max** (register **r2**). The updated value of **max** is shown the **Expressions** window (**Fig.33**).

Expression	Type	Value
> a1	int [5]	0x20000000 <a1>
∨ ➔ pa1	int *	0x20000004 <a1+4>
(x)= *pa1	int	-9
∨ ➔ &pa1	int **	0x20000014 <pa1>
> ➔ *&pa1	int *	0x20000004 <a1+4>
(x)= max	int	12
> ➔ &max	int *	0x20000040 <max>
(x)= i	int	0
> ➔ &i	int *	0x20017ff4

Fig.33

The above **str** instruction initializes the **max** variable with the first element of array **a1**.

At the next step, we will examine how the **for()** loop appears in the **Disassembly** window.

The **for()** loop

for (int i = 1; i < sizeof(a1)/4; i++);

belongs to **Fragments 2** and **5** of disassembly and begins with the following instructions shown in the **Disassembly** window (**Fig.34**).

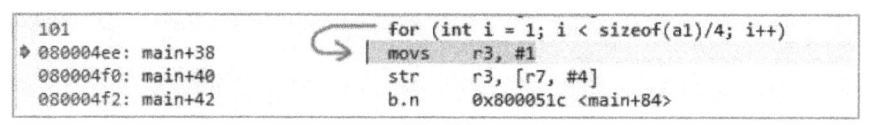

```
101                        for (int i = 1; i < sizeof(a1)/4; i++)
♦ 080004ee: main+38           movs    r3, #1
  080004f0: main+40           str     r3, [r7, #4]
  080004f2: main+42           b.n     0x800051c <main+84>
```
Fig.34

This code fragment is repeated in **Listing 18**.

Listing 18.

                        for (int i = 1; i < sizeof(a1)/4; i++)

080004ee: main+38   movs   r3, #1

```
080004f0: main+40            str     r3, [r7, #4]
080004f2: main+42            b.n     0x800051c <main+84>
```

Note that before the first instruction

```
movs  r3, #1
```

from this sequence is executed, the variable **i** (address 0x20017ff4) is already initialized with 0 as is shown in the **Expressions** window (**Fig.35**).

Expression	Type	Value
> 📁 a1	int [5]	0x20000000 <a1>
> ➡ pa1	int *	0x20000004 <a1+4>
> ➡ &pa1	int **	0x20000014 <pa1>
(x)= max	int	12
> ➡ &max	int *	0x20000040 <max>
(x)= i	int	0
∨ ➡ &i	int *	0x20017ff4
(x)= *&i	int	0

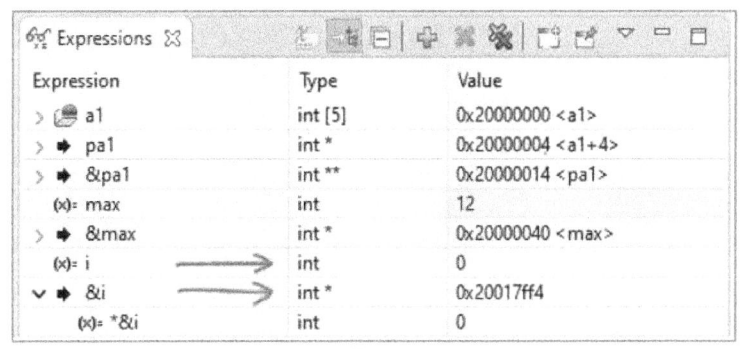

Fig.35

The **for()** loop, however, should begin to run with **i** = 1. Examining the code in **Listing 18**, we can assume that this sequence of 3 MCU instructions will initialize variable **i** with 1.
The first instruction in this sequence

```
080004ee: main+38              movs   r3, #1
```

writes 1 to the core register **r3**.
Before executing the instruction

```
080004f0: main+40              str    r3, [r7, #4]
```

let's look at register **r7** in the **Registers** window (**Fig.36**).

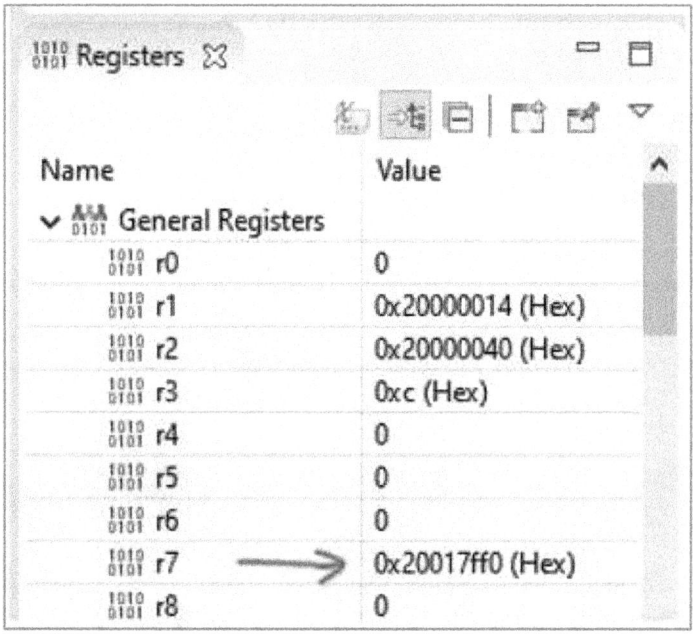

Name	Value
∨ General Registers	
r0	0
r1	0x20000014 (Hex)
r2	0x20000040 (Hex)
r3	0xc (Hex)
r4	0
r5	0
r6	0
r7	⟶ 0x20017ff0 (Hex)
r8	0

Fig.36

It is seen that register **r7** contains the address of the variable **i** less 4. If we analyze the information from **Fig.35** and **Fig.36**, it becomes clear that this **str** instruction will write 1 to the address of variable **i** thus implicitly implementing the assignment operator

i = 1;

After the **str** instruction is executed, the variable **i** is assigned 1 as expected (**Fig.37**).

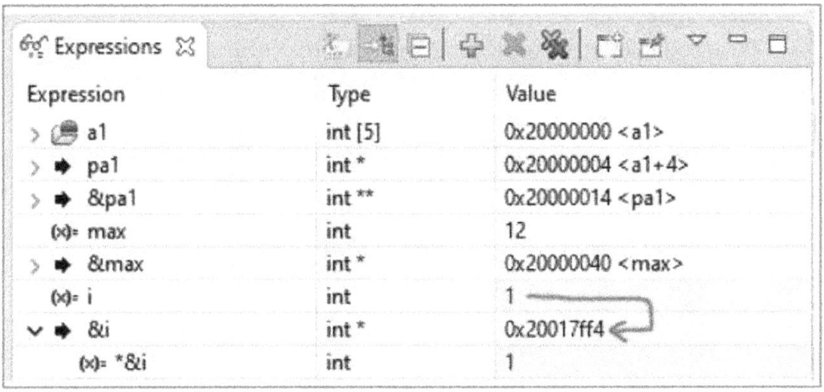

Expression	Type	Value
> a1	int [5]	0x20000000 <a1>
> ➔ pa1	int *	0x20000004 <a1+4>
> ➔ &pa1	int **	0x20000014 <pa1>
(x)= max	int	12
> ➔ &max	int *	0x20000040 <max>
(x)= i	int	1
v ➔ &i	int *	0x20017ff4
(x)= *&i	int	1

Fig.37

Then the branch instruction

080004f2: main+42   b.n   0x800051c <main+84>

causes the next sequence (**Listing 19**) to execute.

Listing 19.

```
0800051c: main+84    ldr    r3, [r7, #4]
0800051e: main+86    cmp    r3, #4
08000520: main+88    bls.n  0x80004f4 <main+44>
```

The above code fragment simply tests the condition

i < sizeof(a1)/4

in the **for()** loop.

If the condition is true, the rest of statements within **for()** will be executed, otherwise the loop terminates.
The **for()** loop increments variable **i** by 1 before the next iteration begins using the sequence shown in **Listing 20**.

Listing 20.

```
08000516: main+78    ldr    r3, [r7, #4]
08000518: main+80    adds   r3, #1
```

```
0800051a: main+82    str    r3, [r7, #4]
0800051c: main+84    ldr    r3, [r7, #4]
0800051e: main+86    cmp    r3, #4
08000520: main+88    bls.n  0x80004f4 <main+44>
```

In this code, the first 3 MCU instructions

```
08000516: main+78    ldr    r3, [r7, #4]
08000518: main+80    adds   r3, #1
0800051a: main+82    str    r3, [r7, #4]
```

increment the loop variable **i** by 1 that corresponds to the high-level statement

i++;

Then the next 3 MCU instructions

```
0800051c: main+84    ldr    r3, [r7, #4]
0800051e: main+86    cmp    r3, #4
08000520: main+88    bls.n  0x80004f4 <main+44>
```

test the condition

i < 5

and branches back to the beginning of the **for()** loop if this condition is true. If the condition is false, the **for()** loop terminates and the endless **while()** loop (**Listing 21**) begins to run.

Listing 21.

```
                     while (1)
08000522: main+90    b.n    0x8000522 <main+90>
```

At this point, I am going to analyze the first statement within the **for()** loop:

if (max < *pa1) max = *pa1;

This statement and corresponding MCU instructions are already named **Fragment 3**. The **if()** statement will be repeated several times, therefore we examine only a single iteration.

In order to simplify analysis of disassembly, I first determine what elementary operations the given code fragment performs.
Breaking down the **if()** statement will give me the following:
1. the value of **max** is loaded from memory to some core MCU register;
2. the value at the address pointed by **pa1** is loaded into some core register;
3. the comparison of both registers is executed and NZCV flags are set accordingly;
4. depending on the NZCV flags, either of two possible low-level sequences will be implemented:
    - **max** ≥ ***pa1**, then the **if()** statement terminates and a new iteration begins;
    - **max** < ***pa1**, then the new value from the register keeping ***pa1** will be stored at the address in memory where **max** is placed. Then a new iteration begins.

In the **Disassembly** window, the **if()** statement is broken down into the following MCU instructions (**Listing 22**).

Listing 22.

```
                        if (max < *pa1) max = *pa1;
080004f4: main+44       ldr     r3, [pc, #44]   ; (0x8000524 <main+92>)
080004f6: main+46       ldr     r3, [r3, #0]
080004f8: main+48       ldr     r2, [r3, #0]
080004fa: main+50       ldr     r3, [pc, #44]   ; (0x8000528 <main+96>)
080004fc: main+52       ldr     r3, [r3, #0]
080004fe: main+54       cmp     r2, r3
08000500: main+56       ble.n   0x800050c <main+68>
08000502: main+58       ldr     r3, [pc, #32]   ; (0x8000524 <main+92>)
08000504: main+60       ldr     r3, [r3, #0]
08000506: main+62       ldr     r3, [r3, #0]
08000508: main+64       ldr     r2, [pc, #28]   ; (0x8000528 <main+96>)
0800050a: main+66       str     r3, [r2, #0]
```

In the above sequence, the first 2 MCU instructions

```
080004f4: main+44      ldr    r3, [pc, #44]  ; (0x8000524 <main+92>)
080004f6: main+46      ldr    r3, [r3, #0]
```

load the current value of the pointer **pa1** into the core register **r3**. The result can be evaluated by comparing the corresponding values in the **Registers** and **Expressions** windows (**Fig.38**). At this point, **pa1** = 0x200000004 that is the address of the current element (=**a1[1]**) of array **a1**.

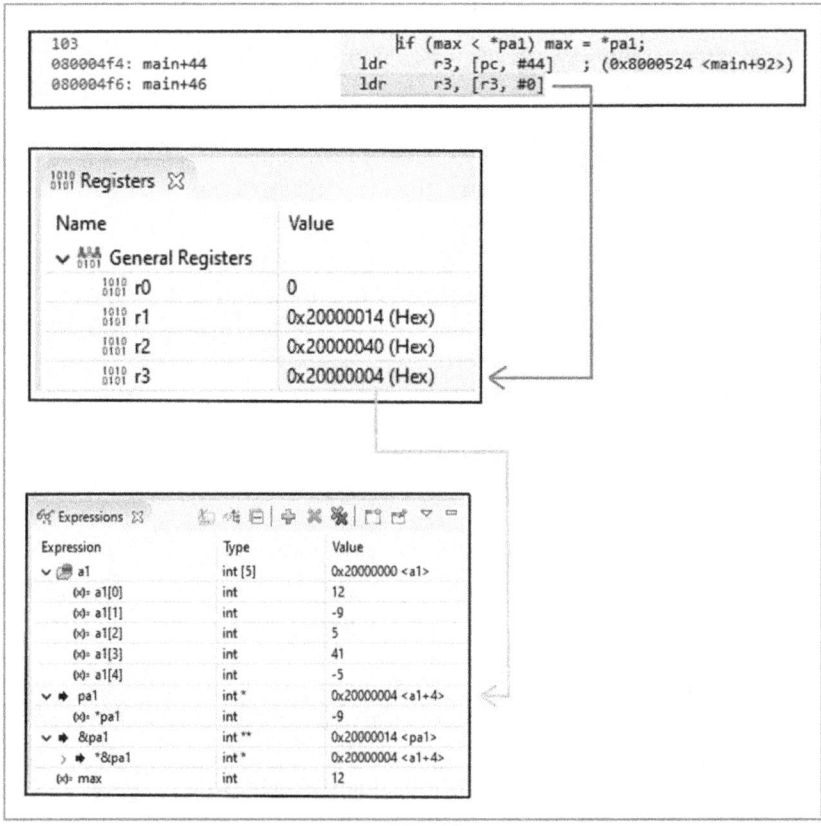

Fig.38

Since **r3** contains the address of the current element of **a1**, I expect that the next MCU instruction(s) will load the value of this element into some core register for further processing.

50

Let's examine the next instruction:

080004f8: main+48   ldr   r2, [r3, #0]

This instruction loads the value of the current element **a1[1]** (=0xfffffff7 or -9) into register **r2**.
The next instruction

080004fa: main+50   ldr   r3, [pc, #44]   ; (0x8000528 <main+96>)

loads the value 0x20000040 that is the address of the **max** variable into register **r3**. This is followed by the instruction

080004fc: main+52   ldr   r3, [r3, #0]

that loads the current value of **max** into register **r3**.
Let's stop here and summarize what we have at this point.
Register **r2** contains 0xfffffff7 (=-9) that is the value of the current element of array **a1** (**a1[1]**). Register **r3** contains the current value of the **max** variable.
As we move to the next two instructions

080004fe: main+54   cmp   r2, r3
08000500: main+56   ble.n   0x800050c <main+68>

it becomes clear that this sequence checks the condition

max ≥ *pa1

Meanwhile, the **if()** statement check the condition

max < *pa1

This illustrates one important thing: at the low level, each ARM compiler can use its original sequence of MCU instructions while implementing some high-level statement. Generally speaking, various compilers may implement the same high-level statement using different sequences of MCU instructions.

51

Comparing the registers **r2** and **r3** affects the NZCV flags in the **xpsr** status register that can be viewed in the **Registers** window. Depending on the result, the instruction

0800050c: main+68   ldr   r3, [pc, #20] ; (0x8000524 <main+92>)

or

08000502: main+58   ldr   r3, [pc, #32] ; (0x8000524 <main+92>)

will be executed.

The branch to the instruction

0800050c: main+68   ldr   r3, [pc, #20] ; (0x8000524 <main+92>)

is taken when the current **max** remains great or equal to the current element of array **a1**. In this case, the current pointer **pa1** is advanced to the next element of array **a1**. This section of disassembly corresponds to **Fragment 4** that we will discuss further.

If it turns out that the current value of **max** is less than the current element of **a1**, the following sequence of MCU instructions (**Listing 23**) begins to run.

Listing 23.

```
08000502: main+58     ldr    r3, [pc, #32]  ; (0x8000524 <main+92>)
08000504: main+60     ldr    r3, [r3, #0]
08000506: main+62     ldr    r3, [r3, #0]
08000508: main+64     ldr    r2, [pc, #28]  ; (0x8000528 <main+96>)
0800050a: main+66     str    r3, [r2, #0]
```

The above sequence replaces the current value stored in variable **max** with the value kept in the current element of array **a1**.
The first 2 instructions in this sequence

```
08000502: main+58     ldr    r3, [pc, #32]  ; (0x8000524 <main+92>)
08000504: main+60     ldr    r3, [r3, #0]
```

load the current pointer **pa1** into register **r3**.
The next instruction

08000506: main+62   ldr   r3, [r3, #0]

loads the element pointed by **pa1** into register **r3**.
At this point, I am almost sure that the next MCU instruction

08000508: main+64   ldr   r2, [pc, #28] ; (0x8000528 <main+96>)

will load the address of **max** into register **r2**. When the instruction is executed, register **r2** will contain 0x20000040 that is the address of variable **max**.
The instruction that follows

0800050a: main+66   str   r3, [r2, #0]

will store the updated value at the address of **max** as expected.
The data flow can be easily traced using the **Registers** and **Expressions** windows (**Fig.39**). The state of variables corresponds to the iteration with variable **i** = 3 when the **max** variable is assigned the updated value = 41 (=0x29).

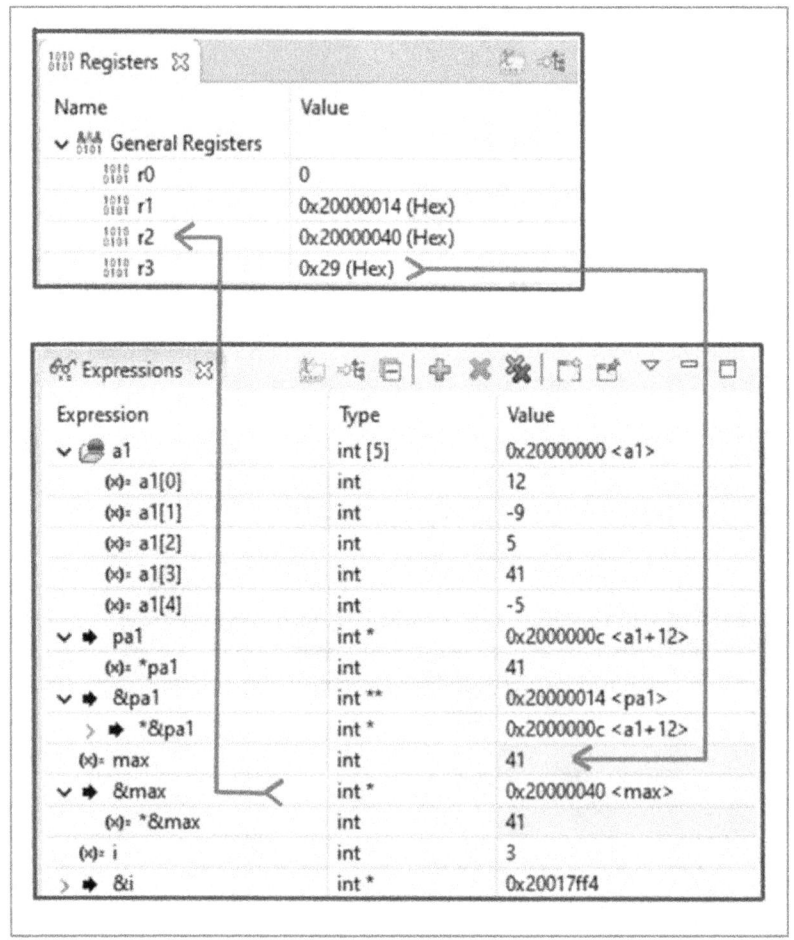

Name	Value
∨ General Registers	
r0	0
r1	0x20000014 (Hex)
r2	0x20000040 (Hex)
r3	0x29 (Hex)

Expression	Type	Value
∨ a1	int [5]	0x20000000 <a1>
a1[0]	int	12
a1[1]	int	-9
a1[2]	int	5
a1[3]	int	41
a1[4]	int	-5
∨ pa1	int *	0x2000000c <a1+12>
*pa1	int	41
∨ &pa1	int **	0x20000014 <pa1>
> *&pa1	int *	0x2000000c <a1+12>
max	int	41
∨ &max	int *	0x20000040 <max>
*&max	int	41
i	int	3
> &i	int *	0x20017ff4

Fig.39

At this point, we finish analyzing **Fragment 3** of disassembly.

The last fragment of disassembly to be analyzed is **Fragment 4**. This fragment (**Listing 24**) simply increments the pointer **pa1** that corresponds to the high-level statement

pa1++;

within the **for()** loop.

Listing 24.

		pa1++;	
0800050c: main+68	ldr	r3, [pc, #20]	; (0x8000524 <main+92>)
0800050e: main+70	ldr	r3, [r3, #0]	
08000510: main+72	adds	r3, #4	
08000512: main+74	ldr	r2, [pc, #16]	; (0x8000524 <main+92>)
08000514: main+76	str	r3, [r2, #0]	

This code fragment is easy to understand and analyze. Since the decompiler gives us a hint about this code fragment, we can assume that after the first 2 MCU instructions

0800050c: main+68	ldr	r3, [pc, #20]	; (0x8000524 <main+92>)
0800050e: main+70	ldr	r3, [r3, #0]	

have been executed, the core register **r3** will contain the pointer **pa1** to the current element of array **a1**. In the iteration with variable **i** = 3, register **r3** should contain the value 0x2000000c (see the **Registers** and **Expressions** windows in **Fig.40**).

Registers

Name	Value
▼ General Registers	
r0	0
r1	0x20000014 (Hex)
r2	0x20000040 (Hex)
r3	0x2000000c (Hex)

Expressions

Expression	Type	Value
▼ a1	int [5]	0x20000000 <a1>
(x)= a1[0]	int	12
(x)= a1[1]	int	-9
(x)= a1[2]	int	5
(x)= a1[3]	int	41
(x)= a1[4]	int	-5
▼ ➡ pa1	int *	0x2000000c <a1+12>
(x)= *pa1	int	41
▼ ➡ &pa1	int **	0x20000014 <pa1>
> ➡ *&pa1	int *	0x2000000c <a1+12>
(x)= max	int	41
▼ ➡ &max	int *	0x20000040 <max>
(x)= *&max	int	41
(x)= i	int	3
> ➡ &i	int *	0x20017ff4

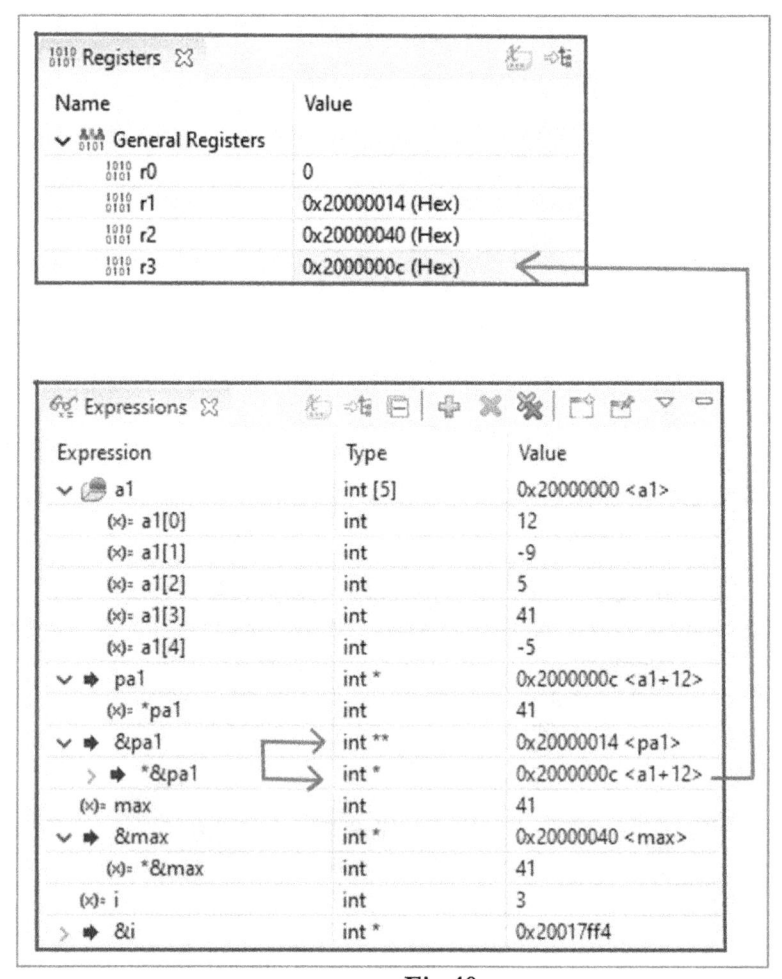

Fig.40

Then the value in **r3** is incremented by 4 (integer is 4 bytes long) using the instruction

08000510: main+72   adds   r3, #4

After executing the instruction, register **r3** will contain 0x20000010.
The next instruction loads the address of pointer **pa1** (=0x20000014) into register **r2**:

08000512: main+74   ldr   r2, [pc, #16] ; (0x8000524 <main+92>)

Finally, the new value of pointer **pa1** is stored at the address placed in register **r2**:

0800050e: main+70   ldr   r3, [r3, #0]

At this point, pointer **pa1** is equal to 0x20000010 (the **Expressions** window, **Fig.41**).

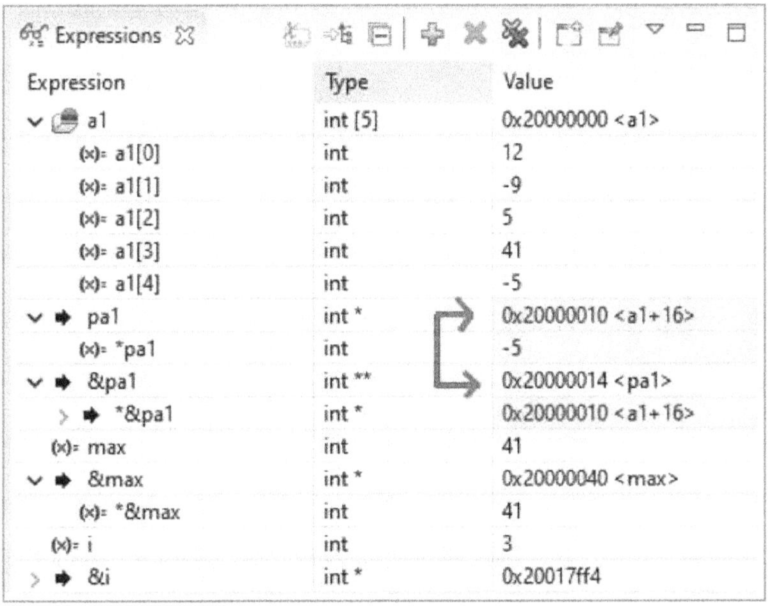

Expression	Type	Value
a1	int [5]	0x20000000 <a1>
(x)= a1[0]	int	12
(x)= a1[1]	int	-9
(x)= a1[2]	int	5
(x)= a1[3]	int	41
(x)= a1[4]	int	-5
pa1	int *	0x20000010 <a1+16>
(x)= *pa1	int	-5
&pa1	int **	0x20000014 <pa1>
*&pa1	int *	0x20000010 <a1+16>
(x)= max	int	41
&max	int *	0x20000040 <max>
(x)= *&max	int	41
(x)= i	int	3
&i	int *	0x20017ff4

Fig.41

At this point we finish analyzing disassembly of our demo code.

Output Data in the Debugger

There may be various ways to output data streams to the console while debugging ARM code in STM32CubeIDE. This section describes a couple of simple methods implementing console output.

Using SWD interface

It is possible to develop a function similar to **printf()** using the ITM port 0 of the SWD interface. This works for Cortex-M processors having the required hardware. Therefore, this method will not work for the Cortex-M0 devices.
Let's create a new STM32 project in STM32CubeIDE and modify the source code of the **main()** function by inserting the following code fragments as is shown in **Listing 25**.

Listing 25.

```
. . . . . . .
#include <stdio.h>

int a1[5] = {1, -5, 9, 2, -7};
int sum_ints = 0;
. . . . . . .

for (int i1 = 0; i1 < sizeof(a1)/4; i1++)
{
 sum_ints += a1[i1];
}
. . . . . . .
```

The above code simply calculates the sum of the elements of an integer array **a1** (variable **sum_ints**). Let's see how to output the current value of **sum_ints** to the console in each iteration of the **for()** loop while debugging.

To do that, we can use the Instrumentation Trace Macrocell (ITM) that allows applications to write arbitrary data to the SWO pin through any of 32 parallel ports. In this case, the data is transmitted from the Cortex-M core to the PC through the JTAG cable. In this example, we will use ITM port 0 to output data to a debug console. Also, we need to use the function

ITM_SendChar(char c)

that takes an ASCII code as a single parameter.
Below (**Listing 26**) is the source code of function **print_data()** that will output the message to the debug console.

Listing 26.

```
int print_data(int num)
{
  char buf[64];
  char *pbuf = buf;
  int bRead;

  bRead = sprintf(buf, "Result = %d\n", num);
  for(int i=0 ; i < bRead; i++)
    ITM_SendChar((*pbuf++));
  return bRead;
}
```

It is seen that the function takes a single parameter that is an integer. The function returns the number of bytes to be written to the console.

When we are done, modify the source code of the **main()** function as is shown in **Listing 27** (the source code just inserted is shown in bold).

Listing 27.

```
#include "main.h"
#include <stdio.h>

int a1[5] = {1, -5, 14, 2, -7};
int sum_ints = 0;
. . . . . . .

/* Private variables ---------------------------------------------------*/
UART_HandleTypeDef huart2;

/* Private function prototypes -----------------------------------------*/
void SystemClock_Config(void);
static void MX_GPIO_Init(void);
static void MX_USART2_UART_Init(void);
int print_data(int num);
. . . . . . .
```

```c
int main(void)
{

    /* Reset of all peripherals, Initializes the Flash interface and the Systick. */
    HAL_Init();

    /* Configure the system clock */
    SystemClock_Config();

    /* Initialize all configured peripherals */
    MX_GPIO_Init();
    MX_USART2_UART_Init();
    . . . . . . .

    for (int i1 = 0; i1 < sizeof(a1)/4; i1++)
    {
      sum_ints += a1[i1];
      print_data(sum_ints);
    }

while (1)
 {

 }
}
. . . . . . .

int print_data(int num)
{
  char buf[64];
  char *pbuf = buf;
  int bRead;

  bRead = sprintf(buf, "Result = %d\n", num);
  for (int i=0 ; i < bRead; i++)
    ITM_SendChar((*pbuf++));
  return bRead;
}
. . . . . . .
```

After the project is build, enter debugging mode and open the
SWV ITM Data Console (**Fig.42**) by clicking
Window → Show View → SWV → SWV ITM Data Console.

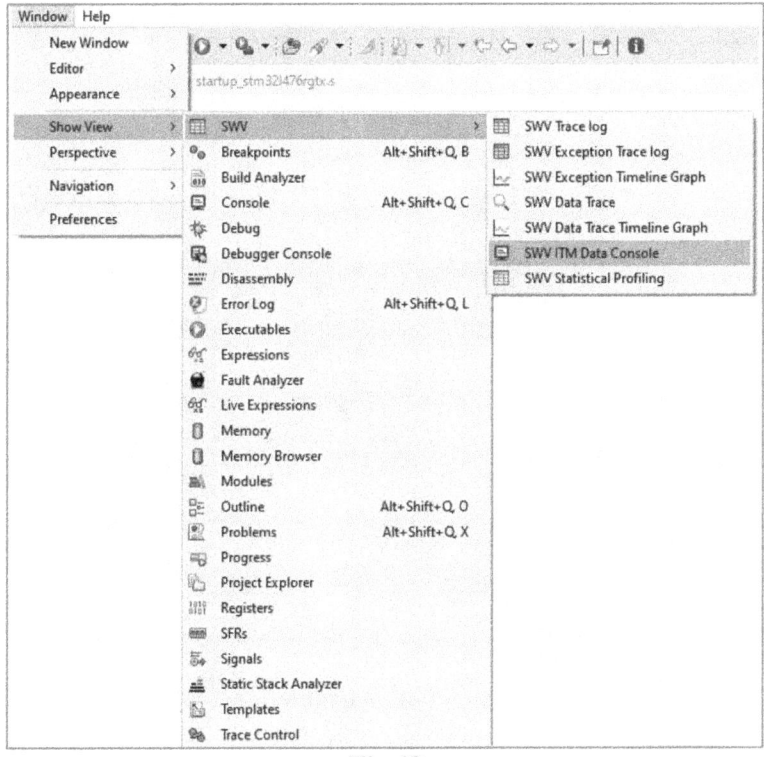

Fig.42

Then we open the configuration window (**Fig.43**) and choose the ITM port 0 (**Fig.44**) while leaving other parameters unchanged.

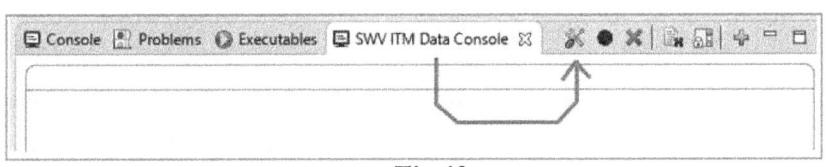

Fig.43

61

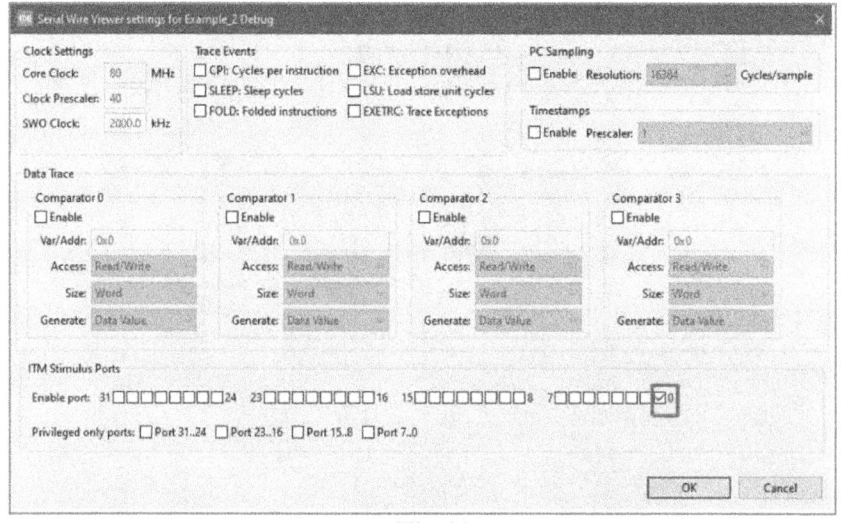

Fig.44

Then we can start tracing by clicking the corresponding icon (**Fig.45**).

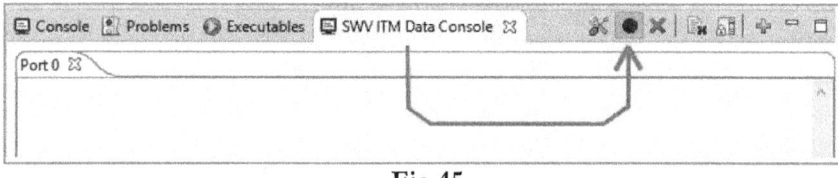

Fig.45

The results of operations are then output through Port 0 (**Fig.46**).

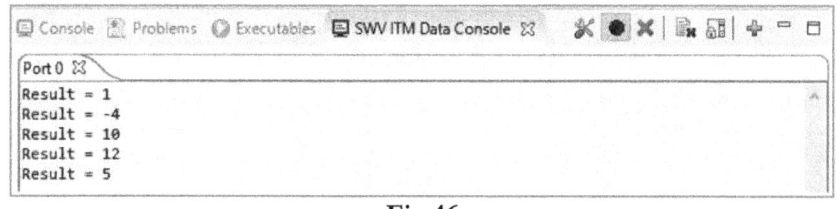

Fig.46

Function **print_data()** can easily be modified to output the floating-point numbers. The source code of the modified function (named **print_fpdata()**) is shown in **Listing 28**.

Listing 28.

```
float print_fpdata(float num)
{
  /* Implement your write code here */
  char buf[64];
  char *pbuf = buf;
  int bRead;

  bRead = sprintf(buf, "Result = %6.3f\n", num);
  for (int i=0 ; i < bRead; i++)
    ITM_SendChar((*pbuf++));
  return bRead;
}
```

The code fragment for testing function **print_fpdata()** is shown in **Listing 29**.

Listing 29.

```
#include <stdio.h>

float a1[5] = {15.8, -53.1, 14.09, 12.99, -7.25};
float sum_fp = 0;
. . . . . . .

for (int i1 = 0; i1 < sizeof(a1)/4; i1++)
  {
        sum_fp += a1[i1];
        print_fpdata(sum_fp);
  }
. . . . . . .
```

Before processing floating-point numbers, we must enable the corresponding options in the Project Settings (**Fig.47**).

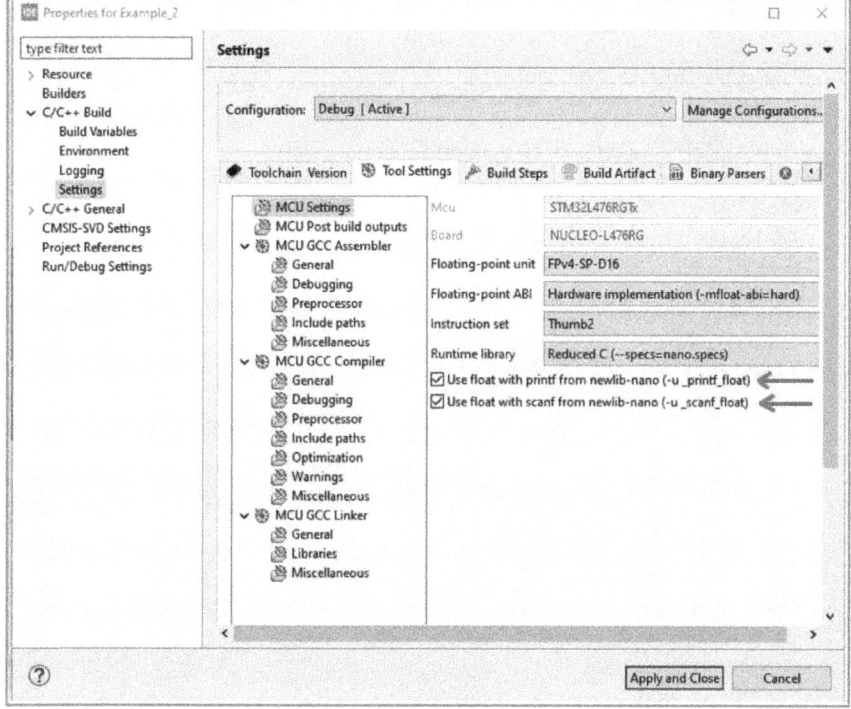

Fig.47

While debugging, the result of operation looks like the following (**Fig.48**).

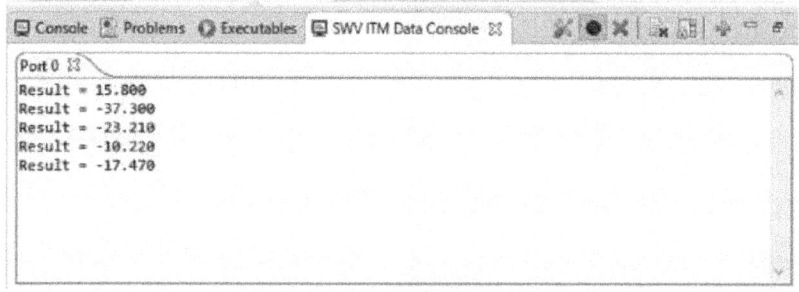

Fig.48

The above examples use the CMSIS macro **ITM_SendChar()** to output a byte of data on the ITM channel (port) 0. It is impossible, however, to use **ITM_SendChar()** to send data on the other ITM channels.

To select any ITM channel 0-31 for data output, we can use low-level access through the ITM data structure that is defined in CMSIS support file **stm32f4xx.h** provided by STM32CubeIDE.

For example, the source code of the **print_data()** function that outputs the sum of integers though ITM channel (port) 2 will look like the following (**Listing 30**).

Listing 30.

```
int print_data(int num)
{
   char buf[64];
   char *pbuf = buf;
   int bRead;

   bRead = sprintf(buf, "Result = %d\n", num);
   for (int i=0 ; i < bRead; i++)
   {
     while (ITM->PORT[2].u32 == 0);
     ITM->PORT[2].u8 = (uint8_t)((*pbuf++));
   }
   return bRead;
}
```

Before using this function in the Debugger, we must choose port 2 as an output channel in the configuration window (**Fig.49**).

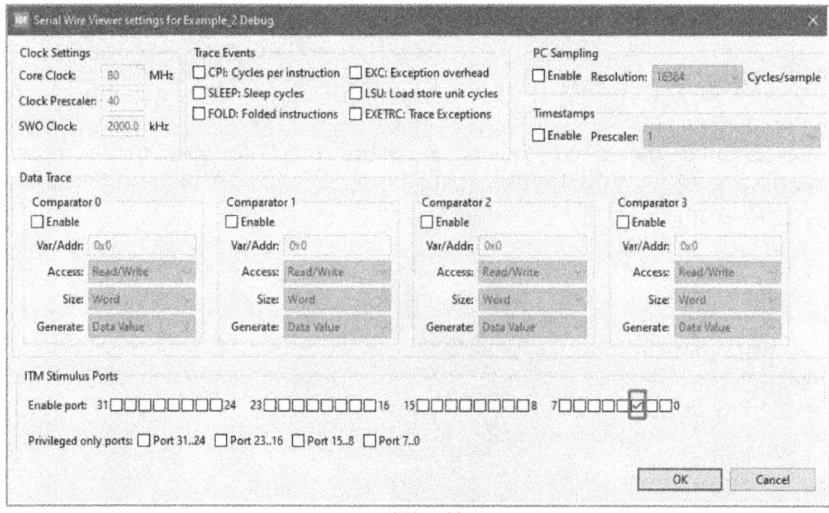

Fig.49

It is also easily to rewrite the source code of the **print_fpdata()** function for floating-point output through ITM port 2 (**Listing 31**).

Listing 31.

```
float print_fpdata(float num)
{
  char buf[64];
  char *pbuf = buf;
  int bRead;

  bRead = sprintf(buf, "Result = %6.3f\n", num);
  for (int i=0 ; i < bRead; i++)
  {
    while (ITM->PORT[2].u32 == 0);
    ITM->PORT[2].u8 = (uint8_t)((*pbuf++));
  }
  return bRead;
}
```

Using USB-UART interface

Besides the ITM interface, it is possible to provide data output to an I/O console using the USB-UART interface. For my NUCLEO-L476RG board, this will be USART2 (**Fig.50**).

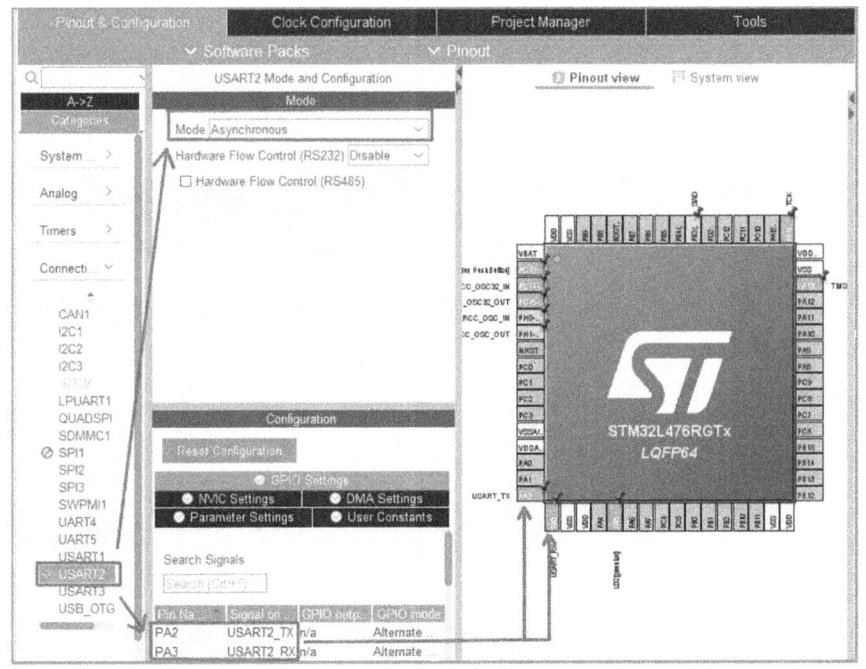

Fig.50

The parameters of USART2 are set on the **Parameter Settings** page (**Fig.51**).

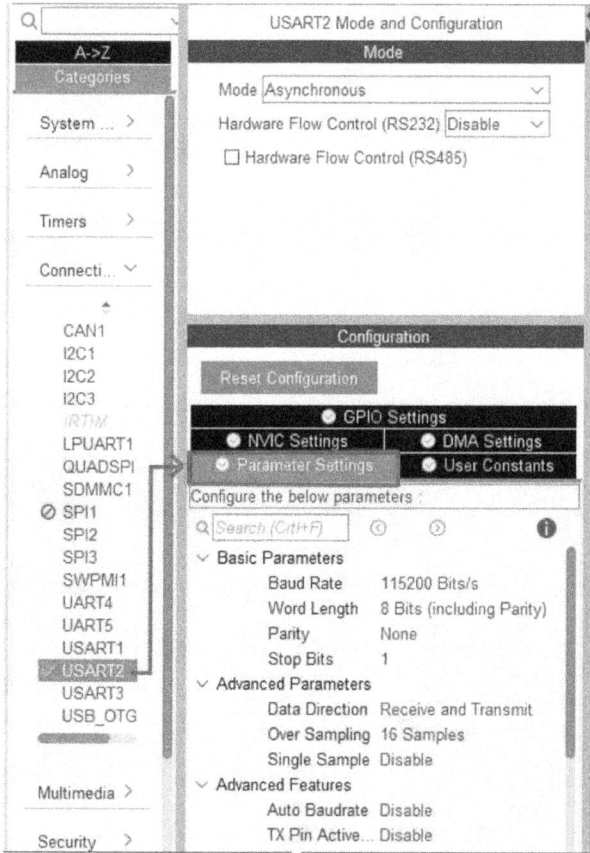

Fig.51

Note that USB-UART interface can be configured after a development board is connected to the USB port on the PC. In my case, USB-UART device appears in Windows 10 as the **STLink Virtual COM port (COM3)** (**Fig.52**).

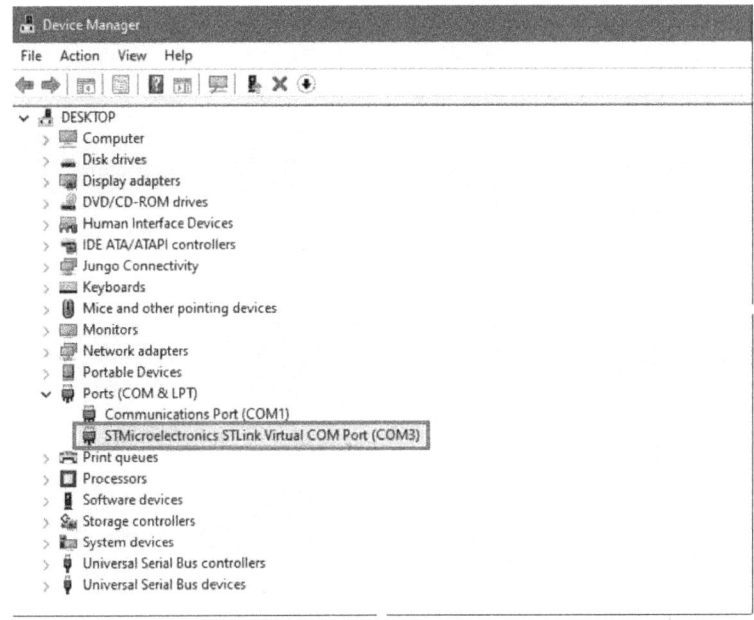

Fig.52

The parameters of the USB-UART device in **Device Manager** of Windows (**Fig.53**) must be the same as those set for an embedded UART (USART2, in my case).

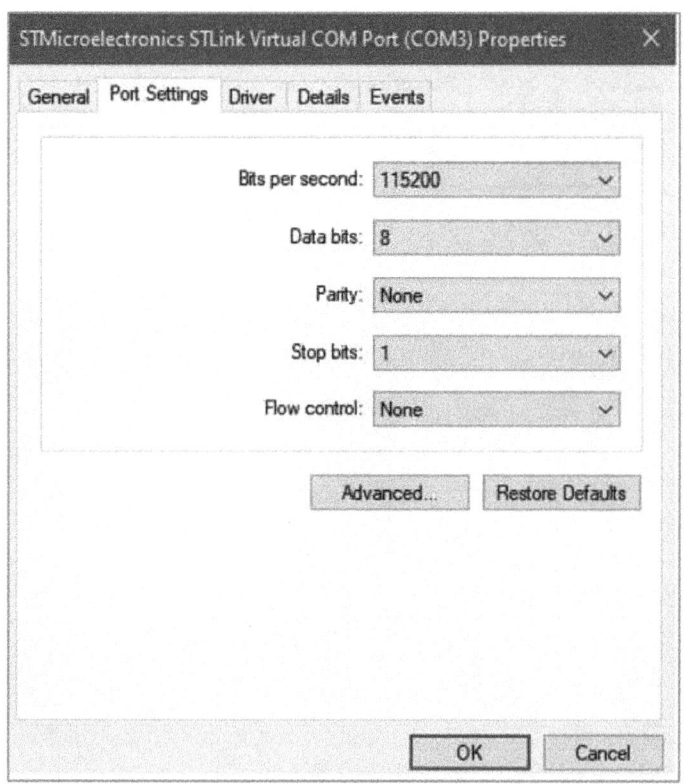

Fig.53

In this example, I use the default parameters for USART2. **Note** that for your particular development board, the configuration settings of USB-UART may be different.
Finally, save the changes and allow the Project wizard to update the source code of a project.

To transfer data to the I/O console, we need some code that will be placed in the function named **print_uart()** (**Listing 32**).

Listing 32.

```
void print_uart(int num)
{
 char buf[64];
 int bRead;
```

```
bRead = sprint (buf, "Result = %d\n\r", num);
HAL_UART_Transmit(&huart2, (uint8_t*)buf, bRead, 300);
}
```

Below (**Listing 33**) is a source code of the **main()** function that uses **print_uart()** to output the sum of elements of an integer array **a1**.

Listing 33.

```
#include "main.h"
#include <stdio.h>
int a1[5] = {-7, 22, 9, -18, 3};
int sum = 0;
. . . . . . .

/* Private variables ---------------------------------------------------------*/
UART_HandleTypeDef huart2;

/* Private function prototypes -----------------------------------------------*/
void SystemClock_Config(void);
static void MX_GPIO_Init(void);
static void MX_USART2_UART_Init(void);
void print_uart(int num);
. . . . . . .

int main(void)
{
  /* Reset of all peripherals, Initializes the Flash interface and the Systick. */
  HAL_Init();

  /* Configure the system clock */
  SystemClock_Config();

  /* Initialize all configured peripherals */
  MX_GPIO_Init();
  MX_USART2_UART_Init();
  . . . . . . .

  for (int i = 0; i < sizeof(a1)/4; i++)
  {
```

```
    sum += a1[i];
    print_uart(sum);
  }

  while (1)
  {

  }
}
. . . . . . .

void print_uart(int num)
{
  char buf[64];
  int bRead;
  bRead = sprintf(buf, "Result = %d\n\r", num);
  HAL_UART_Transmit(&huart2, (uint8_t*)buf, bRead, 300);
}
```

When the debugging session is started, we first need to configure the new I/O console to view the data transmitted through the USB-UART bridge. On the right side of the **Console** window, choose **Open Console** → **Command Shell Console (Fig.54)**.

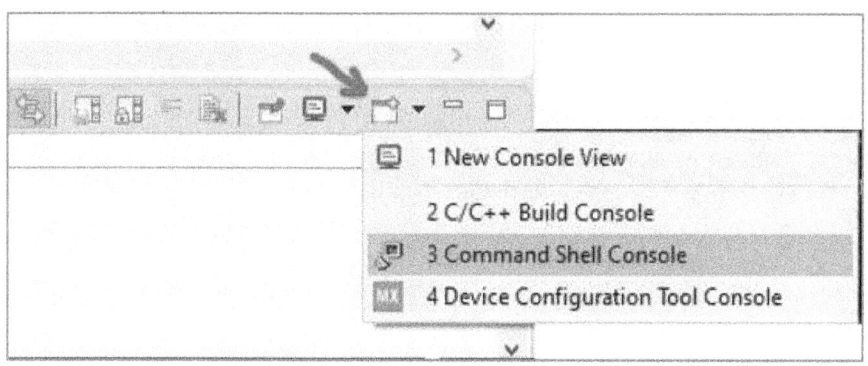

Fig.54

The **Select Remote Connection** window (**Fig.55**) appears.

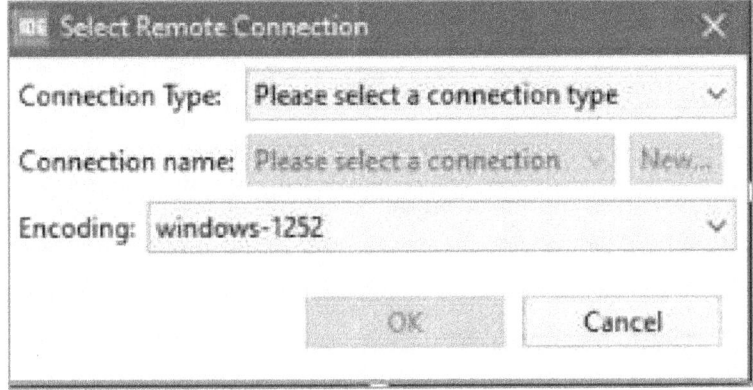

Fig.55

In this window, we should choose the **Serial Port** as a connection type (**Fig.56**).

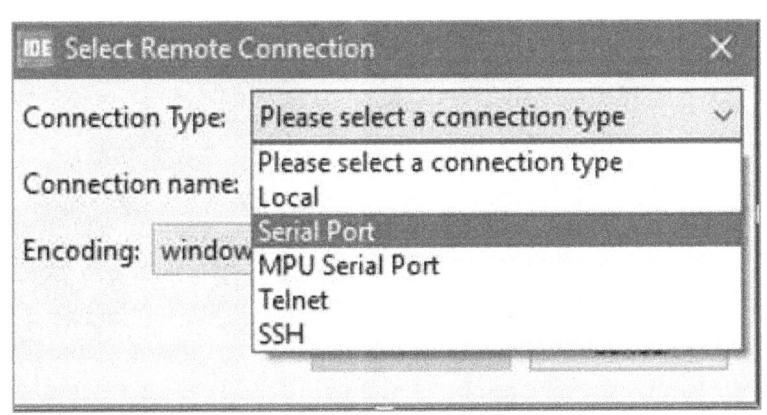

Fig.56

Then click **New…** (**Fig.57**).

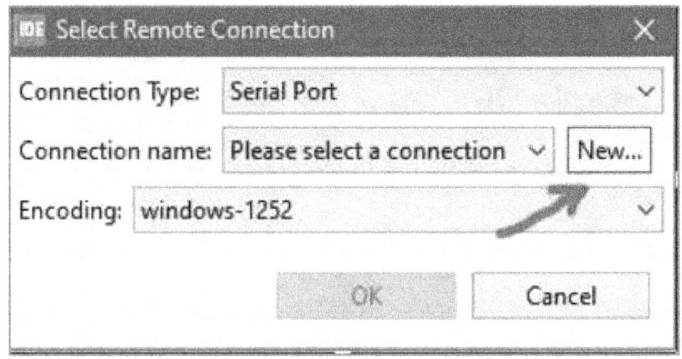

Fig.57

This brings me to the next window (**Fig.58**) where I should set the parameters of the connection.

Fig.58

In my case, the ST Link USB-UART bridge appears as the serial port **COM3** that I name **USB_UART**.
Clicking **Finish** brings me to the next window, where I need to click **OK** to establish the connection (**Fig.59 – Fig.60**).

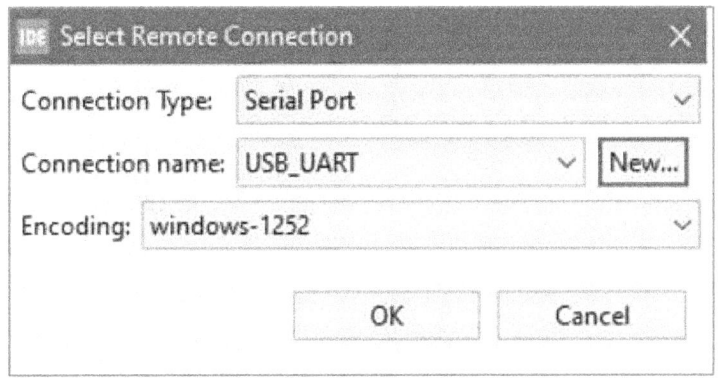

Fig.59

Fig.60

The console output through USB-UART will then look like the following (**Fig.61**).

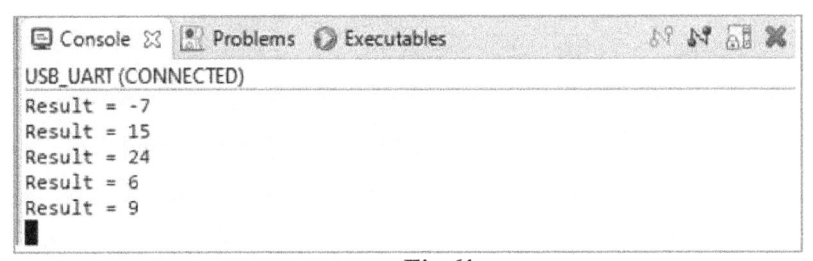

```
USB_UART (CONNECTED)
Result = -7
Result = 15
Result = 24
Result = 6
Result = 9
```

Fig.61

Programmable Breakpoints

If we are interested in examining code / data in some particular point, we usually stop execution using a breakpoint. To set a breakpoint on an instruction, we use either the **Source** or **Disassembly** window while debugging code. Additionally, we can insert a breakpoint instruction into the code to stop program execution when some condition is true.

Example 1

Assume our code will be calculating the sum of integers in some array until 0 is found. When this occurs, we want to stop execution. The code fragment from the **main()** function implementing this algorithm is very simple (**Listing 34**).

Listing 34.

```
int a1[10] = {1, 3, 5, 7, 9, 0, 13, 15, 17, 19};
int sum = 0;
. . . . . . .
int main(void)
{
. . . . . . .
for (int i1 = 0; i1 < sizeof(a1)/4; i1++)
  {
    if (a1[i1] != 0) sum += a1[i1];
    else __asm("BKPT #0\n");
  }
. . . . . . .
while (1)
  {
    /* USER CODE END WHILE */
    HAL_Delay(2000);
    /* USER CODE BEGIN 3 */
  }
. . . . . .
```

Here the MCU instruction

BKPT #0

causes the processor to enter Debug state after element **a1[5]** has been examined. If debugging is running before **BKPT** is invoked, code execution is stopped until we relaunch debugging.

Example 2

This example illustrates the optimized version of the previous code where a **for()** loop is written in Inline Assembler (**Listing 35**).

Listing 35.

```
. . . . . . .
int a1[10] = {1, 3, 5, 7, 0, 11, 13, 15, 17, 19};
int sum = 0;
int size_a1 = sizeof(a1)/4;
. . . . . . .
int main(void)
{
. . . . . . .
__asm (
        "ldr    r0, =a1\n"
        "ldr    r1, =size_a1\n"
        "ldr    r1, [r1]\n"
        "ldr    r2, =0\n"  // the cur. sum = 0
  "next:\n"
        "ldr    r3, [r0], #4\n"
        "cmp    r3, #0\n"
        "ble    stop\n"
        "ittt   gt\n"
        "addgt  r2, r2, r3\n"
        "subsgt r1, r1, #1\n"
        "bgt    next\n"
        "ldr    r0, =sum\n"
        "str    r2, [r0]\n"
        "b      exit\n"
  "stop:\n"
        "bkpt   #0\n"
  "exit:\n"
        "nop\n"
```

);
. . . .

Handling Exceptions

The Cortex-M processors support interrupts and system exceptions. The processor and the Nested Vectored Interrupt Controller (NVIC) handle all exceptions according to their priorities.
The exceptions may be generated by core, floating-point unit (FPU), peripheral devices, etc. When triggered, an exception changes the normal flow of software control. In this case, the processor suspends the current task being executed and executes the fragment of code called the exception handler. After the exception handler terminates, the processor then resumes normal program execution.
When we write the code, we should consider that some exceptions(s) may occur while an application is running. It would be worth to detect most common exceptions (faults) and process them during debugging.
The following examples illustrate how to write the demo code processing some exception and place this code in the corresponding Exception Handler. This demo code will simply output an error message to the console, although it is possible to implement more complicated algorithms for processing exceptions.

Example 1

This demo example allows to handle the <**Divide by 0**> exception within our code. To process an exception, we need to modify the code within the corresponding exception handler located in file **stm32l4xx_it.c**.
In this example, we will intentionally perform the operation of dividing by 0 and then output the message to the console using the exception handler.

Let's create a new STM32 Project with default settings. Then modify the source code generated by STM32CubeIDE for the **main.c** and **stm32l4xx_it.c** files so that to simulate the situation of <**Divide by 0**>. Below (**Listing 36**) is the modified code of the **main()** function. The inserted lines are shown in bold.

Listing 36.

```c
#include "main.h"
#include <stdio.h>

int a1[5] = {4, -8, 3, 7, 2};
int a2[5] = {2, -1, 0, 4, 9};
. . . . . . .

/* Private variables ---------------------------------------------------------*/
UART_HandleTypeDef huart2;

/* Private function prototypes -----------------------------------------------*/
void SystemClock_Config(void);
static void MX_GPIO_Init(void);
static void MX_USART2_UART_Init(void);
void print_data(uint32_t num);
. . . . . . .

int main(void)
{

  /* Configure the system clock */
  SystemClock_Config();

  /* Initialize all configured peripherals */
  MX_GPIO_Init();
  MX_USART2_UART_Init();

  for (int i1 = 0; i1 < sizeof(a1)/4; i1++)
        a1[i1] = a1[i1]/a2[i1];

  while (1)
  {
  }
}

void print_data(uint32_t num)
{
  char buf[64];
  int bRead;
```

```
bRead = sprintf (buf, "Exception Code = 0x%X\n\r", (int)num);
HAL_UART_Transmit(&huart2, (uint8_t*)buf, bRead, 300);
}
```

In this code, the elements of an integer array **a1** are divided by the elements of array **a2** in the **for()** loop. Function **print_data()** that outputs the exception code to the console is called from the **HardFault_Handler()** exception handler (file **stm32l4xx_it.c**). We inserted a few lines of code (shown in bold in **Listing 37**) into this handler to output the exception code on the USB-UART console.

Listing 37.

```
void HardFault_Handler(void)
{
  /* USER CODE BEGIN HardFault_IRQn 0 */

  faultCode = SCB->CFSR;
  print_data(faultCode);

  /* USER CODE END HardFault_IRQn 0 */
  while (1)
  {
    /* USER CODE BEGIN W1_HardFault_IRQn 0 */
    /* USER CODE END W1_HardFault_IRQn 0 */
  }
}
```

Also, we need to add the following definitions (shown in bold in **Listing 38**) at the beginning of code in the **stm32l4xx_it.c** file.

Listing 38.

```
#include "main.h"
#include "stm32l4xx_it.h"
volatile uint32_t faultCode;
extern void print_data(uint32_t num);
```

To determine the fault, we check the Configurable Fault Status Register CFSR of the System Control Block (SCB). SCB is the programmer's model interface to the processor. It provides system implementation information

and system control, including configuration, control, and reporting of system exceptions.
When the <**Divide by 0**> exception is triggered, bit 25 in the Usage Fault Status subregister (UFSR) of CFSR will be set (=1) (**Fig.62**).

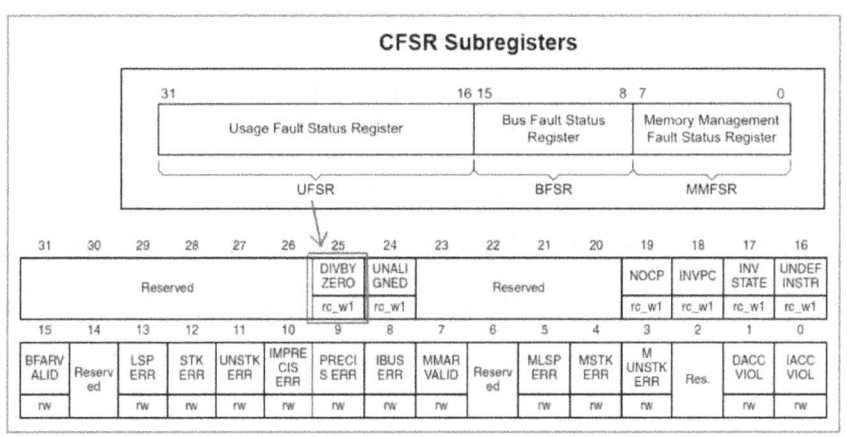

Fig.62

When we are done, build project and launch the Debugger. Then add the command shell console (in my case, I use USB-UART bridge build around UART2 interface of NUCLEO-L476RG).
If we single-step through the instructions in debugging mode, we reach the point where element **a1[2]** is divided by **a2[2]** - this raises the <**Divide by 0**> exception that launches the **HardFault_Handler()**.
When this exception is triggered, bit 25 (DIVBYZERO) in the Usage Fault Status subregister (UFSR) is set. The value of UFSR is then output to the console window (**Fig.63**).

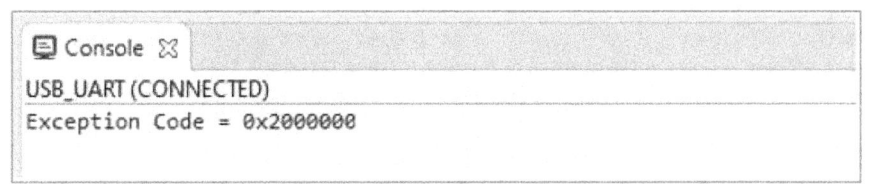

```
Console
USB_UART (CONNECTED)
Exception Code = 0x2000000
```

Fig.63

This value can further be examined if needed.

Example 2

This is one more example that illustrates how to write the code to process the <**No Coprocessor Usage Fault, NOCP**> exception within your application. The NOCP exception occurs when access to a coprocessor (FPU) is denied.

The FPU is disabled from reset and we must enable it before using any floating-point instructions. The STM32CubeIDE Code Generator enables FPU while configuring peripherals with their default mode. To illustrate processing the NOCP exception, we will disable FPU at some point and write the code for an exception handler.

When the **NOCP** exception is triggered, bit 19 (NOCP) in the Usage Fault Status subregister (UFSR) of CFSR will be set (=1) (**Fig.64**). We can check this bit within the **HardFault_Handler()** exception handler by modifying the handler code. As in the previous example, our exception handler will simply output the data to the console.

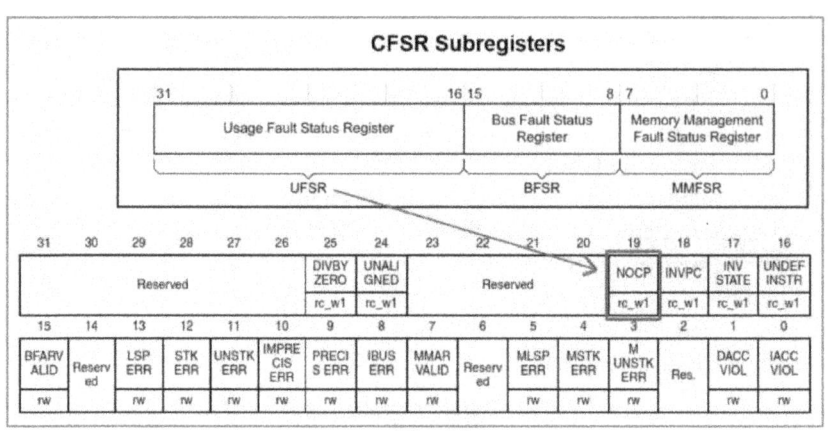

Fig.64

Let's create a new STM32 Project with default settings and modify the source code in the files **main.c** and **stm32l4xx_it.c** so that to simulate the **NOCP** exception.

The source code of the **main()** function will then look like the following (**Listing 39**).

Listing 39.

```c
#include "main.h"
#include <stdio.h>
#include <math.h>

int a1[5] = {4, 56, 3, 27, 2};
float b1[5];
. . . . . . .

/* Private variables ---------------------------------------------------------*/
UART_HandleTypeDef huart2;
. . . . . . .

/* Private function prototypes -----------------------------------------------*/
void SystemClock_Config(void);
static void MX_GPIO_Init(void);
static void MX_USART2_UART_Init(void);
void print_data(uint32_t num);
. . . . . . .

int main(void)
{
  /* Reset of all peripherals, Initializes the Flash interface and the Systick. */
  HAL_Init();

  /* Configure the system clock */
  SystemClock_Config();

  /* Initialize all configured peripherals */
  MX_GPIO_Init();
  MX_USART2_UART_Init();

  for (int i1 = 0; i1 < sizeof(a1)/4; i1++)
  {
  if (i1 == 3)
     __asm (
        "ldr    r0, =0xE000ED88\n"
        "ldr    r1, [r0]\n"
        "bfc    r1, #20, #4\n"
        "str    r1, [r0]\n"
        "dsb\n"
```

```
        "isb\n"
      );
    b1[i1] = sqrt(a1[i1]);
}

while (1)
  {
  }
}

void print_data(uint32_t num)
{
  char buf[64];
  int bRead;
  bRead = sprint (buf, "Exception Code = 0x%X\n\r", (int)num);
  HAL_UART_Transmit (&huart2, (uint8_t*)buf, bRead, 300);
}
. . . . . . .
```

In this code, the sequence in the **for()** loop calculates the square root of the elements of array a1 and writes the result into array b1. When index **i1 = 3**, the Inline Assembler code **disables** the FPU by clearing bits 20-23 in the Coprocessor Access Control Register (CPACR) whose address is 0xE000ED88 (**Fig.65**).

4.6.1 Coprocessor access control register (CPACR)

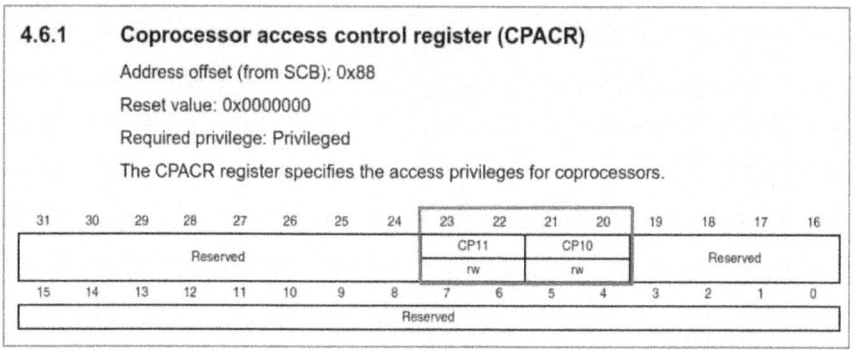

Address offset (from SCB): 0x88

Reset value: 0x0000000

Required privilege: Privileged

The CPACR register specifies the access privileges for coprocessors.

31	30	29	28	27	26	25	24	23	22	21	20	19	18	17	16
			Reserved					CP11 rw		CP10 rw			Reserved		
15	14	13	12	11	10	9	8	7	6	5	4	3	2	1	0
								Reserved							

Fig.65

Disabling the FPU will raise the **HardFault** exception that will be processed by the **HardFault_Handler()** exception handler. We will modify the source code of the **HardFault_Handler()** so that to output the exception code to the console.

To do that, we modify the source code of the **HardFault_Handler()** exception handler (file **stm32l4xx_it.c**). This code will be the same as that shown in **Listing 37** from **Example 1**. For convenience, this source code is repeated in **Listing 40**.

Listing 40.

```
void HardFault_Handler(void)
{
  /* USER CODE BEGIN HardFault_IRQn 0 */

  faultCode = SCB->CFSR;
  print_data(faultCode);

  /* USER CODE END HardFault_IRQn 0 */
  while (1)
  {
    /* USER CODE BEGIN W1_HardFault_IRQn 0 */
    /* USER CODE END W1_HardFault_IRQn 0 */
  }
}
```

Recall that function **print_data()** outputs the exception code to the console. Also, the following definitions (shown in bold in **Listing 41**) should be added to the beginning of the source code in **stm32l4xx_it.c**.

Listing 41.

```
#include "main.h"
#include "stm32l4xx_it.h"
volatile uint32_t faultCode;
extern void print_data(uint32_t num);
```

After the project is built without errors, launch the Debugger and single-step through the instructions. At some point, when index **i1** becomes equal to 3, the Inline Assembler code fragment disables the FPU. Then when the code tries to access the FPU, the **NOCP** exception is triggered. The exception handler code then outputs the exception code (**Fig.66**) that can further be examined.

```
Console
USB_UART (CONNECTED)
Exception Code = 0x80000
```

Fig.66

Example 3

This is one more example that illustrates processing hard fault error. As usual, we will simulate hardware error by inserting the necessary code into **main.c**. Also we will modify the source code of the **HardFault_Handler()** exception handler in file **stm32l4xx_it.c**.
In **main.c**, we make the following changes (**Listing 42**).

Listing 42.

#include "main.h"
#include <stdio.h>
. . . .

void print_data(uint32_t num);
void SystemClock_Config(void);
static void MX_GPIO_Init(void);
static void MX_USART2_UART_Init(void);
. . . .

int main(void)
{
. . . .

HAL_Init();

/* Configure the system clock */

```c
  SystemClock_Config();

  /* Initialize all configured peripherals */
  MX_GPIO_Init();
  MX_USART2_UART_Init();
  . . . . . . .

  __asm (
        "ldr    r0, =0xFFF\n"
        "push   {r0}\n"
        "pop    {pc}\n"
  );

  while (1)
  {
  }
}

void print_data(uint32_t num)
{
  char buf[64];
  int bRead;
  bRead = sprintf (buf, "Exception Code = 0x%X\n\r", (int)num);
  HAL_UART_Transmit(&huart2, (uint8_t*)buf, bRead, 300);
}
```

In the above code, we simulate hardware error by executing the **__asm()** block of code.

In the **stm32l4xx_it.c** file, we should add the definitions and modify the source code of the **HardFault_Handler()** exception handler as is shown in **Listing 43**.

Listing 43.

```c
volatile uint32_t faultCode;
extern void print_data(uint32_t num);
. . . . . . .

void HardFault_Handler(void)
```

```
{
/* USER CODE BEGIN HardFault_IRQn 0 */
faultCode = SCB->HFSR;
print_data(faultCode);

/* USER CODE END HardFault_IRQn 0 */
while (1)
{
  /* USER CODE BEGIN W1_HardFault_IRQn 0 */
  /* USER CODE END W1_HardFault_IRQn 0 */
}
}
```

When this exception is triggered, bit 30 in the Hard Fault Status register (HFSR) is set (**Fig.67**).

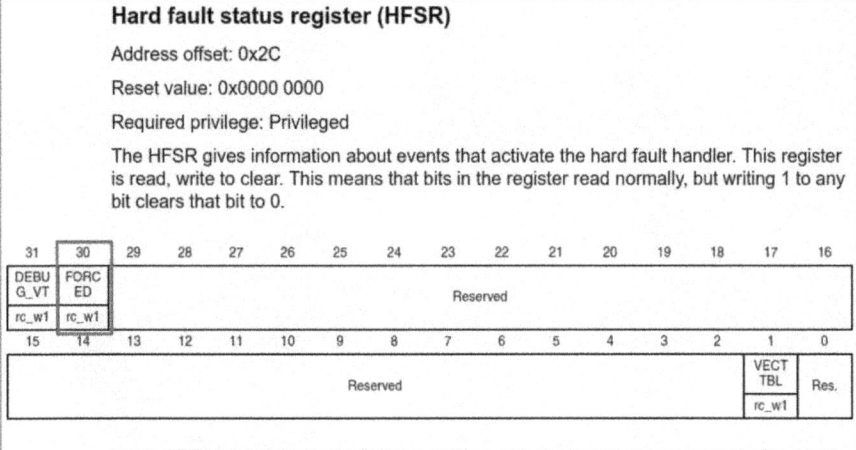

Hard fault status register (HFSR)

Address offset: 0x2C

Reset value: 0x0000 0000

Required privilege: Privileged

The HFSR gives information about events that activate the hard fault handler. This register is read, write to clear. This means that bits in the register read normally, but writing 1 to any bit clears that bit to 0.

31	30	29	28	27	26	25	24	23	22	21	20	19	18	17	16
DEBUG_VT	FORCED							Reserved							
rc_w1	rc_w1														

15	14	13	12	11	10	9	8	7	6	5	4	3	2	1	0
							Reserved							VECT TBL	Res.
														rc_w1	

Bit 31 DEBUG_VT: Reserved for Debug use. When writing to the register you must write 0 to this bit, otherwise behavior is unpredictable.

Bit 30 FORCED: Forced hard fault. Indicates a forced hard fault, generated by escalation of a fault with configurable priority that cannot be handles, either because of priority or because it is disabled.
When this bit is set to 1, the hard fault handler must read the other fault status registers to find the cause of the fault.
0: No forced hard fault
1: Forced hard fault.

Fig.67

While in debugging mode, when the exception is triggered, the **HardFault_Handler()** code outputs the value of register HFSR to the console (**Fig.68**).

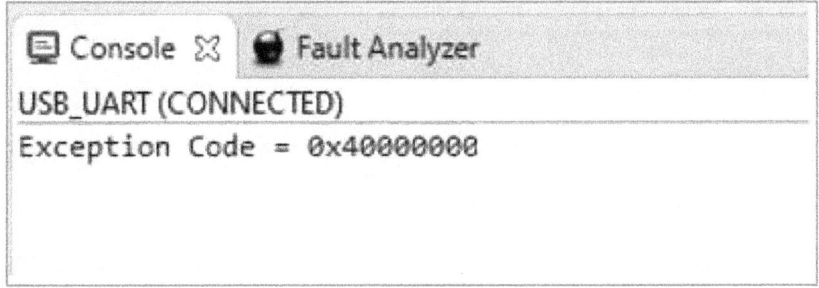

```
Console   Fault Analyzer
USB_UART (CONNECTED)
Exception Code = 0x40000000
```

Fig.68

Using Supervisor Calls

The supervisor call (SVC) is an exception that is used by the ARM Cortex-M processor core to perform privileged operations. Usually, embedded application code runs at the unprivileged level, therefore some hardware resources are inaccessible.
If the embedded code tries to directly access some protected resources, this causes an access violation thus leading to an exception (fault). In order to access to the protected resources, the supervisor call (SVC) mechanism is used. For example, SVC comes in handy, when the program code needs to access special registers that can only be accessed in privileged mode.
The Cortex-M cores support the supervisor call (SVC) instruction that can trigger an exception. A developer can place the SVC instruction somewhere within the code to invoke the exception handler as a to implement some operation.
The following demo examples illustrate how to use SVC.

Example 1

When we begin to write code for processing SVC, we can use the template code for SVC exception handler (named **SVC_Handler()**) generated by

STM32CubeIDE while creating an STM32 project. This code is included in file **stm32l4xx_it.c** and looks like the following (**Listing 44**).

Listing 44.

```
void SVC_Handler(void)
{
  /* USER CODE BEGIN SVCall_IRQn 0 */

  /* USER CODE END SVCall_IRQn 0 */
  /* USER CODE BEGIN SVCall_IRQn 1 */

  /* USER CODE END SVCall_IRQn 1 */
}
```

We will use this template for writing our code for **SVC_Handler()**, but before doing this, we first need to examine the template code in low level. To do that, we will insert a couple of lines (shown in bold in **Listing 45**) into the **main ()** function and build the project.

Listing 45.

```
int main(void)
{
  . . . . . . .
  HAL_Delay(100);
  __asm("SVC #3\n");
  while (1)
  {
    /* USER CODE END WHILE */

    /* USER CODE BEGIN 3 */
  }
  /* USER CODE END 3 */
}
  . . . . . . .
```

In this code, the instruction

SVC #3

when invoked raises the SVC exception with number 3 thus causing the **SVC_Handler()** exception handler to execute.

After the project is built without errors, launch the Debugger and step through the code until the **"SVC #3"** instruction begins executing. At this point, the exception is raised and the processor begins to execute the **SVC_Handler()** code. When we examine the **Disassembly** window, we will see only the prologue and epilogue code of the **SVC_Handler()** (**Listing 46**).

Listing 46.

```
                        SVC_Handler:
080007f2: SVC_Handler+0      push    {r7}
080007f4: SVC_Handler+2      add     r7, sp, #0
. . . . . . .
080007f6: SVC_Handler+4      nop
080007f8: SVC_Handler+6      mov     sp, r7
080007fa: SVC_Handler+8      ldr.w   r7, [sp], #4
080007fe: SVC_Handler+12     bx      lr
```

When invoked, our **SVC_Handler()** exception handler does nothing because we didn't insert any additional code. Also, the SVC number (=3, in our case) embedded into the **SVC** instruction means nothing to the **SVC_Handler()**.

Let's write the code that will make the **SVC_Handler()** much more useful. This code should extract the SVC number from the stack frame and take appropriate action. Note that additional parameters can also be extracted from the stack as well.

First, modify the **main()** source code by inserting a few lines of code (shown in bold, **Listing 47**).

Listing 47.

```
while (1)
{
   /* USER CODE END WHILE */
   HAL_Delay(100);
   __asm("SVC #3\n");
```

```
HAL_Delay(100);
__asm("SVC #19\n");
HAL_Delay(100);
__asm("SVC #171\n");
  /* USER CODE BEGIN 3 */
}
```

In this code fragment, we invoke the **SVC** instruction with 3 different numbers within **a while (1)** loop. After SVC is executed, the **SVC_Handler()** exception handler should return the value of SVC number in the core register **r0**, therefore we modify the **SVC_Handler()** source code as is shown in **Listing 48**.

Listing 48.

```
void SVC_Handler(void)
{
  /* USER CODE BEGIN SVCall_IRQn 0 */
  __asm (
        "mrs    r0, msp\n"
        "ldr    r0, [r0, #28]\n"
        "ldr    r0, [r0, #-2]\n"
        "and    r0, r0, #0xff\n"
  );
  /* USER CODE END SVCall_IRQn 0 */
  /* USER CODE BEGIN SVCall_IRQn 1 */

  /* USER CODE END SVCall_IRQn 1 */
}
```

In this code, we use the Inline Assembler **__asm** block. The instruction

    mrs   r0, msp

moves the contents of a main stack pointer (**msp**) to a core register **r0**. **Note** that in Handler mode, the processor uses main stack pointer. Then we will be capable of retrieving the SVC number from **r0** using the following sequence:

    ldr   r0, [r0, #28]
    ldr   r0, [r0, #-2]

When the **SVC_Handler()** is invoked, the processor pushes the registers **r0**-**r3**, **r12** and **lr** onto the stack. As usual, the return address is stored in the link register (**lr**). All these registers occupy 4x6 = 24 bytes. Additionally, the prolog code (see **Listing 46**) pushes register **r7** onto the stack that takes extra 4 bytes. Therefore, in order to read the stacked PC value into register **r0**, we use the instruction

ldr   r0, [r0, #28]

Since we have the PC value in **r0**, it is easily to read the SVC instruction and its number into **r0** by executing the following instruction

ldr   r0, [r0, #-2]

The SVC number is stored in lower byte of the instruction, therefore the next instruction

and   r0, r0, #0xff

leaves only the value of a low byte in register **r0**. Thus, we will have the SVC number in register **r0**. We can trace how register **r0** is updated by viewing the **Registers** window while debugging the application.

Example 2

This example illustrates how to use an SVC number to perform a few operations. Actually, we will execute the **SVC** instruction with two different numbers to enable / disable Timer 6 (TIM6) interrupts.
Let's create a new STM32 Project with peripherals configured with their default mode. Since I use NUCLEO-L476RG board, I choose SYSCLK = 80 MHz and pin **PA5** (the LED network) configured as output.
The configuration page of Timer 6 is shown in **Fig.69**.

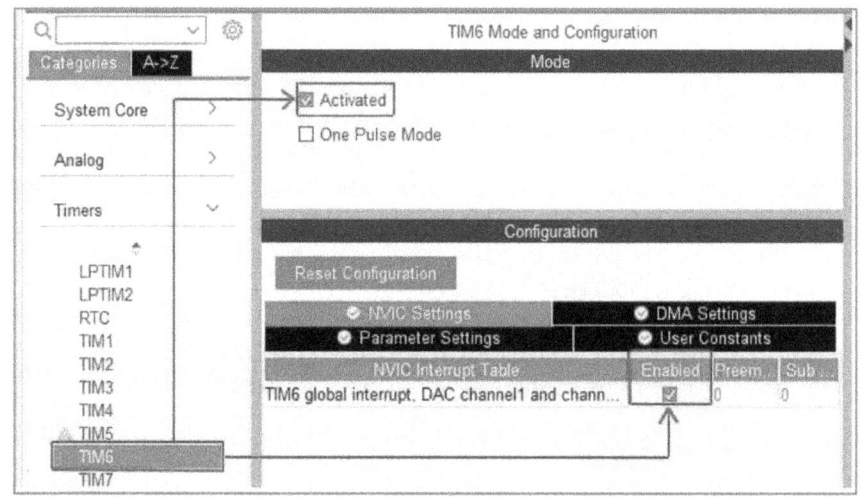

Fig.69

Here we only check the **Activated** and **Enabled** check boxes. The rest of the TIM6 parameters will be configured after the STM32CubeIDE Code Generator has finished its job.

First, open the **main()** function and modify the source code of the **MX_TIM6_Init()** function that initializes Timer 6. To do that, we need to insert a few lines of code () (shown in bold in **Listing 49**) into **MX_TIM6_Init()**.

Listing 49.

```
static void MX_TIM6_Init(void)
{
. . . . . . .
  htim6.Instance = TIM6;
  htim6.Init.Prescaler = 40000;
  htim6.Init.CounterMode = TIM_COUNTERMODE_UP;
  htim6.Init.Period = 400;
. . . . . . .

  HAL_TIM_Base_Start_IT(&htim6);
}
```

In this code, the statements

htim6.Init.Prescaler = 40000;
htim6.Init.Period = 400;

set the frequency of Timer 6 overflowing equal to 5 Hz:

80 MHz / 40000 / 400 = 5 Hz (Period = 1/5Hz = 0.2 s)

The statement

HAL_TIM_Base_Start_IT(&htim6);

starts Timer 6 counting.
Next, configure the TIM6 Interrupt Handler code (function **TIM6_DAC_IRQHandler()** in file **stm32l4xx_it.c**) so that the on-board LED can be toggled when the TIM6 interrupt is triggered. The modified source code of **TIM6_DAC_IRQHandler()** is shown in **Listing 50**.

Listing 50.

```
void TIM6_DAC_IRQHandler(void)
{
  /* USER CODE BEGIN TIM6_DAC_IRQn 0 */

  /* USER CODE END TIM6_DAC_IRQn 0 */
  HAL_TIM_IRQHandler(&htim6);

  /* USER CODE BEGIN TIM6_DAC_IRQn 1 */

  HAL_GPIO_TogglePin(GPIOA, GPIO_PIN_5);

  /* USER CODE END TIM6_DAC_IRQn 1 */
}
```

When we are done with Timer 6, insert a few lines of code into the **while (1)** loop (shown in bold in **Listing 51**).

Listing 51.

```
while (1)
{
```

```
HAL_Delay(10000);
__asm("svc #5\n"); // disable TIM6 INT
HAL_Delay(10000);
__asm("svc #9\n"); // enable TIM6 INT
}
```

Here the instruction

svc #5

will disable the Timer 6 interrupt. Conversely, the instruction

svc #9

will enable the Timer 6 interrupt.
The above code fragment will drive the on-board LED ON/OFF every 10 s. Finally, we need to modify the **SVC_Handler()** code in file **stm32l4xx_it.c** as is shown in **Listing 52**.

Listing 52.

```
void SVC_Handler(void)
{
  /* USER CODE BEGIN SVCall_IRQn 0 */
    __asm (
        ".global HAL_NVIC_DisableIRQ\n"
        ".global HAL_NVIC_EnableIRQ\n"
        "mrs    r0, msp\n"
        "ldr    r0, [r0, #28]\n"
        "ldr    r0, [r0, #-2]\n"
        "and    r0, r0, #0xff\n"
        "teq    r0, #5\n"
        "bne    next\n"
        "push   {lr}\n"
        "mov    r0, #54\n"
        "bl     HAL_NVIC_DisableIRQ\n"
        "pop    {lr}\n"
        "b      exit\n"
    "next:\n"
        "teq    r0, #9\n"
```

```
        "bne     exit\n"
        "push    {lr}\n"
        "mov     r0, #54\n"
        "bl      HAL_NVIC_EnableIRQ\n"
        "pop     {lr}\n"
    "exit:\n"
        );
  /* USER CODE END SVCall_IRQn 0 */
  /* USER CODE BEGIN SVCall_IRQn 1 */

  /* USER CODE END SVCall_IRQn 1 */
}
```

To implement the control over Timer 6 interrupt, we use the __asm block. To enable/disable interrupts, it would be convenient to use the API functions **HAL_NVIC_EnableIRQ()** and **HAL_NVIC_DisableIRQ()** respectively. To access both functions, we need to declare them using the "**.global**" directive. Both functions take a single parameter (the number of an interrupt) in the core register **r0** that. Since the Timer 6 interrupt number is 54, we store this parameter in register **r0** immediately before any of these functions is called.

To determine what action (enabling or disabling the interrupt) should be taken, the SVC number is evaluated using one of the instructions

```
teq    r0, #5
teq    r0, #9
```

Retrieving the SVC number is implemented by the sequence

```
mrs    r0, msp
ldr    r0, [r0, #28]
ldr    r0, [r0, #-2]
and    r0, r0, #0xff
```

This sequence was already described when we analyzed Example 1. Since this code runs in Handler mode, we use the main stack pointer (**msp**).

Understanding STM32 peripherals

The Cortex-M microcontrollers contain the rich sets of peripherals for interfacing with the external world (General-Purpose Input-Output (GPIO) ports, Timers, Analog-To-Digital Converters (ADC), Digital-To-Analog Converters (DAC), etc.).

Debugging peripherals of embedded microcontroller (MCU) may seem difficult enough for software engineers and programmers because of complexity of MCU architecture. and may take a long time. Therefore, it may be nice to highlight a few key principles concerning peripheral device operations rather than overloading your brain with numerous and redundant details. These principles are described in this section.

Accessing peripheral devices

As we already know, all operations on data (addition, subtraction, multiplication, division, shifting, etc.) in ARM microcontrollers are performed using the MCU core registers **r0 – r12**.

This means that there will be no direct data transfer between two memory locations. Also, no data can be processed at some memory location. If, for example, the program code should check the state of some GPIO pin, it is first needed to load the address of a corresponding GPIO port into some core register, then read the data located at this address into a core register for further analyzing.

To control peripherals such as digital input/output ports/pins (GPIO), timers, Analog-To-Digital converters, etc. the **memory-mapped** registers are used. Each peripheral device has its own set of unique registers.

After a microcontroller is powered on or reset, all peripheral devices are put in some predetermined states. A developer must consider these states when writing a code.

Peripheral device interfaces

Basically, reading / writing data from / to peripheral devices are implemented by MCU through interfaces called "busses". This is illustrated in **Fig.70** that represents a very simple hypothetical system with a Cortex-M processor having only two most common types of peripherals – GPIO and Timers.

Cortex-M MCU

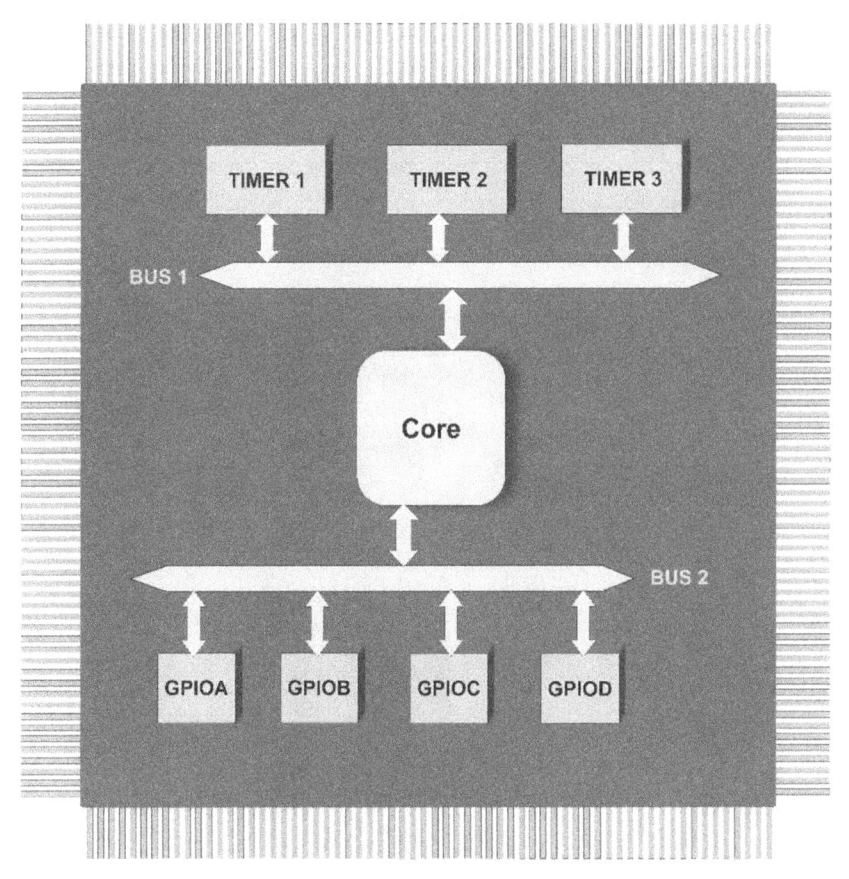

Fig.70

Different peripheral devices may operate with different speed, therefore a Cortex-M microcontroller provides various buses for various devices. In our case, timers **Timer 1 – Timer 3** are controlled through **BUS 1**, while I/O ports **GPIOA – GPIOD** are controlled though **BUS 2**.

Reading and writing data with peripherals

The control of peripheral devices in ARM microcontrollers is provided through a memory-mapped registers. Each peripheral device has its own set of registers whose addresses occupy some dedicated region in memory. The ARM microcontroller when runs some code knows nothing about GPIO, Timers and other devices – it "sees" only the memory region associated with each device.

Let's modify our hypothetical Cortex-M system shown in the block diagram in **Fig.70** so that to reflect this principle. Then our system will look like the following (**Fig.71**).

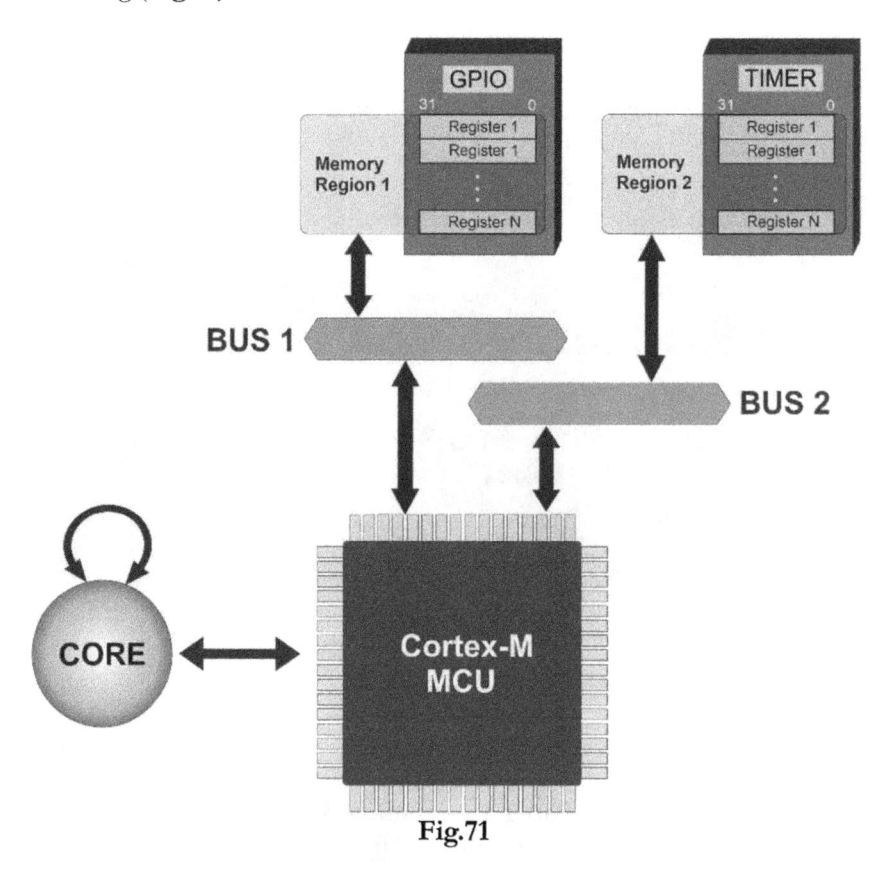

Fig.71

The following excerpt from a datasheet on the STM32L476xx MCU (**Fig.72**) shows the memory regions (boundary addresses) occupied by a few peripheral devices (GPIOs, RNG and ADC).

Table 1. STM32L475xx/476xx/486xx devices memory map and peripheral register boundary addresses

Bus	Boundary address	Size (bytes)	Peripheral	Peripheral register map
AHB2	0x5006 0800 - 0x5006 0BFF	1 KB	RNG	Section 27.8.4: RNG register map
	0x5006 0400 - 0x5006 07FF	1 KB	Reserved	-
	0x5006 0000 - 0x5006 03FF	1 KB	AES	Section 28.7.18: AES register map
	0x5004 0400 - 0x5005 FFFF	127 KB	Reserved	-
	0x5004 0000 - 0x5004 03FF	1 KB	ADC	Section 18.7.4: ADC register map on page 615
	0x5000 0000 - 0x5003 FFFF	256 KB	OTG_FS	Section 47.15.54: OTG_FS register map
	0x4800 2000 - 0x4FFF FFFF	~127 MB	Reserved	-
	0x4800 1C00 - 0x4800 1FFF	1 KB	GPIOH	Section 8.4.13: GPIO register map
	0x4800 1800 - 0x4800 1BFF	1 KB	GPIOG	Section 8.4.13: GPIO register map
	0x4800 1400 - 0x4800 17FF	1 KB	GPIOF	Section 8.4.13: GPIO register map
	0x4800 1000 - 0x4800 13FF	1 KB	GPIOE	Section 8.4.13: GPIO register map
	0x4800 0C00 - 0x4800 0FFF	1 KB	GPIOD	Section 8.4.13: GPIO register map
	0x4800 0800 - 0x4800 0BFF	1 KB	GPIOC	Section 8.4.13: GPIO register map
	0x4800 0400 - 0x4800 07FF	1 KB	GPIOB	Section 8.4.13: GPIO register map
	0x4800 0000 - 0x4800 03FF	1 KB	GPIOA	Section 8.4.13: GPIO register map

Fig.72

We can easily reach and control any peripheral device knowing its boundary address. For example, to write data into some output pin of port **GPIOA**, our code should first refer to register **GPIO_ODR** whose address is calculated as a [**base address + offset**]. The base address of **GPIOA** is 0x4800 0000 (**1** in **Fig.72**) and the offset for register **GPIO_ODR** is 0x14. Therefore, the address where to write data will be [0x4800 0000 + 0x10]. For most devices (timers, A/D converters, etc.), we also need to know the speed of data transfer that depends on the bus (**AHB2**, in our example) where a particular device is attached to (**2** in **Fig.72**).

Clocking peripherals

All core and peripheral devices of microcontrollers can operate only if they are clocked.
This principle is illustrated by the simplest sequential logic circuit shown in **Fig.73**.

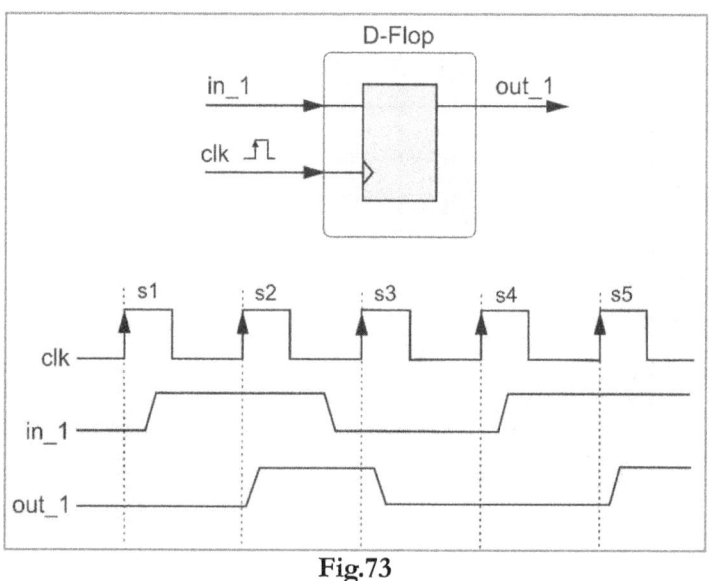

Fig.73

This shows the 1-bit logic element called D-Flop. Such element with various modifications is a fundamental block of any microcontroller/microprocessor system. All registers and memory devices in a microcontroller consist of a various types and numbers of D-Flops.

As is illustrated in the timing diagram, signal **in_1** will appear on output **out_1** only if some edge (rising one, in this example) of the clocking signal **clk** arrives at the clock input. The **in_1** signal may be either from a microcontroller (write operation) or some input source such as GPIO or memory (read operation). Again, the output signal **out_1** may be fed to some GPIO, memory or processor. No data will be transferred from input to output while the clock **clk** is inactive.

STM32Fxx microcontrollers have complex clocking systems feeding all core and peripheral devices. It may take some time and efforts to understand how such system is organized. Nevertheless, to start programming it is enough to know a few basic facts about the STM32 MCU clocking systems.

The microcontroller must provide different clocks for different buses for operating core and peripheral device. For STM32 Cortex-M microcontrollers, all these clocks are derived from the system clock (SYSCLK). SYSCLK, in turn, can be configured using either of the following clock sources:
- HSI oscillator clock;
- HSE oscillator clock;
- Main PLL (PLL) clock.

The high-speed external clock signal (HSE) can be generated from two possible clock sources, HSE external crystal/ceramic resonator or HSE external user clock. The HSE has the advantage of producing a very accurate rate on the main clock.
The HSI clock signal is generated from an internal 16 MHz RC oscillator and can be used directly as a system clock, or used as PLL input.
The HSI RC oscillator has the advantage of providing a clock source at low cost (no external components). It also has a faster startup time than the HSE crystal oscillator however, even with calibration the frequency is less accurate than an external crystal oscillator or ceramic resonator.

A main PLL (PLL) clocked by the HSE or HSI oscillator is used to generate the high-speed system clock.
Let's modify our hypothetical system shown in **Fig.71** by introducing the system clock SYSCLK. The modified block diagram of our system will then look like the following (**Fig.74**).

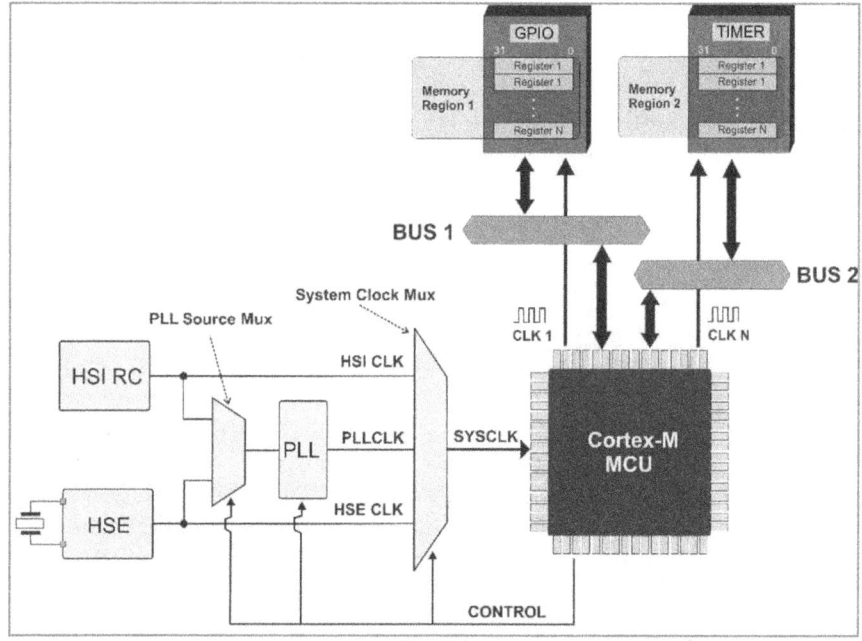

Fig.74

After a system reset, the HSI oscillator is selected as the system clock. When a clock source is used directly or through PLL as the system clock, it is not possible to stop it.

Enabling and disabling peripheral devices

Each peripheral device can be stopped or started by disabling/enabling the clock feeding this device. If clocking to the particular devices is disabled, such device is stopped and we aren't capable to read/write the new data from/to the device any more.
Note, however, that the data previously written into a device are kept unchanged even if clocking is disabled (this is illustrated in the timing diagram in **Fig.73**).
The very simplified block diagram (**Fig.75**) illustrates how the peripheral devices can be clocked.

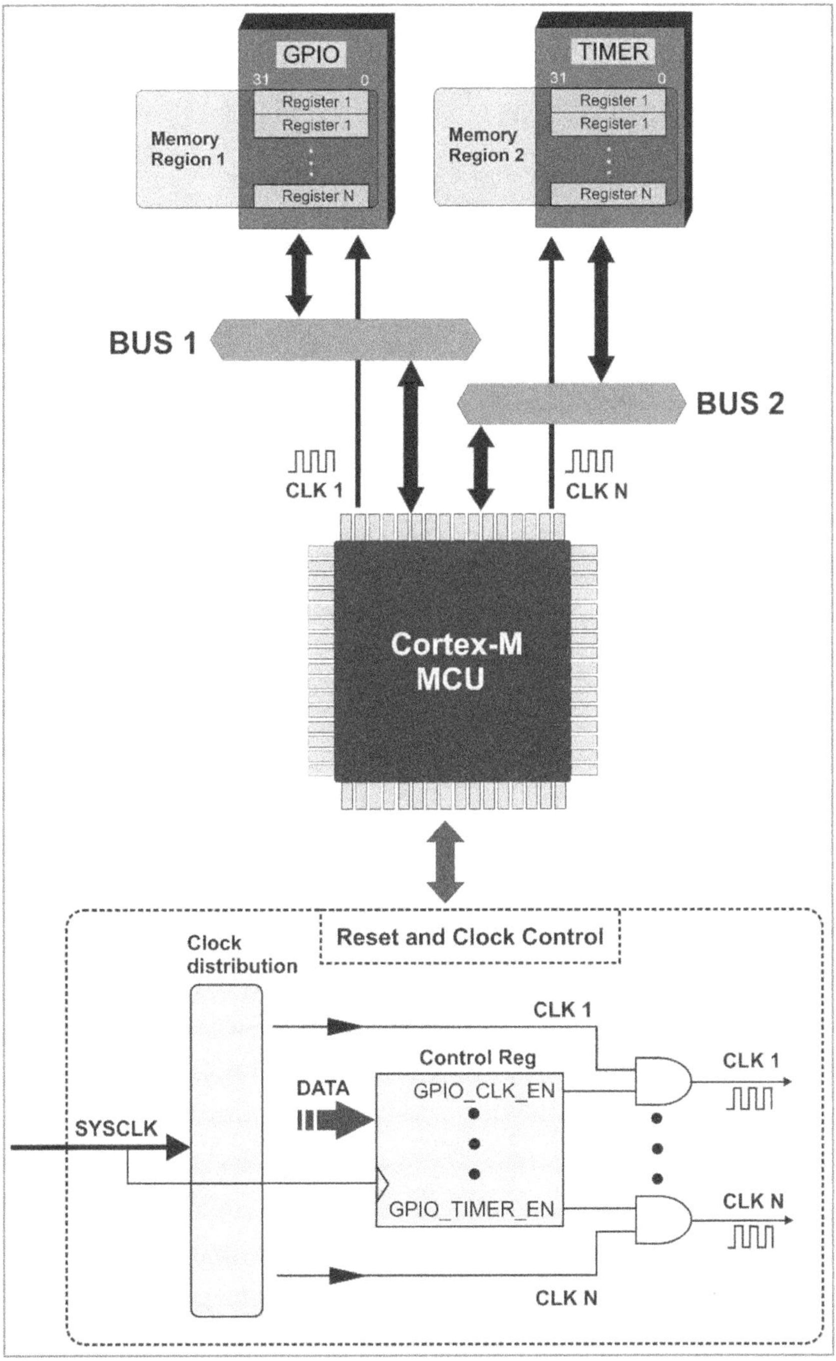

GPIO
31
0
Register 1
Register 1
Register N
Memory Region 1
TIMER
31
0
Register 1
Register 1
Register N
Memory Region 2
BUS 1
BUS 2
CLK 1
CLK N
Cortex-M MCU
Reset and Clock Control
Clock distribution
CLK 1
Control Reg
DATA
GPIO_CLK_EN
CLK 1
SYSCLK
GPIO_TIMER_EN
CLK N
CLK N

Fig.75

Handling Interrupts

As an embedded developer, you will frequently face with exceptions ("interrupts") generated by peripheral devices. Interrupts are usually generated from peripheral or external inputs, timers and in some cases, they can be triggered by software. The exception handlers processing interrupts are also referred to as Interrupt Service Routines (ISR).
Real-time applications usually require to immediately process interrupts that may occur at random time. To provide this, the microcontroller has an interrupt system that should be configured to process interrupts.
Each microcontroller provides processing interrupts through the subsystem whose main part is Nested Vectored Interrupt Controller (NVIC). Now, our demo microcontroller system may look like the following (**Fig.76**).

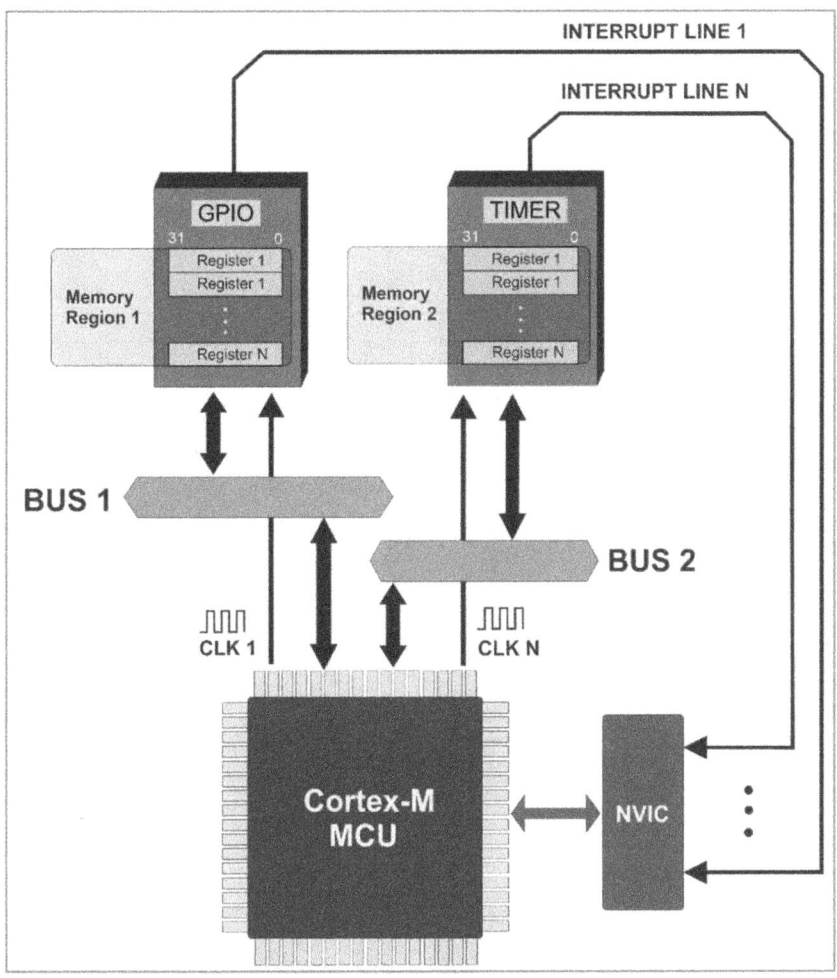

Fig.76

The NVIC and the processor core interface are closely coupled, which enables low latency interrupt processing and efficient processing of late arriving interrupts. All interrupts including the core exceptions are managed by the NVIC.

Pin alternate functions

Each microcontroller has a limited number of pins, while peripherals usually require much more pins than available. For that reason, every pin may be configured to perform a few alternate functions. For example, some GPIO pin can be used as digital output, digital input, PWM output or analog input to A/D converter depending on design.

Below (**Fig.77**) is the excerpt from the datasheet on STM32L4xx microcontrollers where a few alternate functions for GPIO port A are described.

Port		AF0	AF1	AF2	AF3	AF4	AF5	AF6	AF7
Port		SYS_AF	TIM1/TIM2/ TIM5/TIM8/ LPTIM1	TIM1/TIM2/ TIM3/TIM4/ TIM5	TIM8	I2C1/I2C2/I2C3	SPI1/SPI2	SPI3/DFSDM	USART1/ USART2/ USART3
Port A	PA0	-	TIM2_CH1	TIM5_CH1	TIM8_ETR	-	-	-	USART2_CTS
	PA1	-	TIM2_CH2	TIM5_CH2	-	-	-	-	USART2_RTS_DE
	PA2	-	TIM2_CH3	TIM5_CH3	-	-	-	-	USART2_TX
	PA3	-	TIM2_CH4	TIM5_CH4	-	-	-	-	USART2_RX
	PA4	-	-	-	-	-	SPI1_NSS	SPI3_NSS	USART2_CK
	PA5	-	TIM2_CH1	TIM2_ETR	TIM8_CH1N	-	SPI1_SCK	-	-
	PA6	-	TIM1_BKIN	TIM3_CH1	TIM8_BKIN	-	SPI1_MISO	-	USART3_CTS
	PA7	-	TIM1_CH1N	TIM3_CH2	TIM8_CH1N	-	SPI1_MOSI	-	-
	PA8	MCO	TIM1_CH1	-	-	-	-	-	USART1_CK
	PA9	-	TIM1_CH2	-	-	-	-	-	USART1_TX
	PA10	-	TIM1_CH3	-	-	-	-	-	USART1_RX
	PA11	-	TIM1_CH4	TIM1_BKIN2	-	-	-	-	USART1_CTS
	PA12	-	TIM1_ETR	-	-	-	-	-	USART1_RTS_DE
	PA13	JTMS-SWDIO	IR_OUT	-	-	-	-	-	-
	PA14	JTCK-SWCLK	-	-	-	-	-	-	-
	PA15	JTDI	TIM2_CH1	TIM2_ETR	-	-	SPI1_NSS	SPI3_NSS	-

Fig.77

That is what we need to know before programming and debugging peripheral devices.

Debugging GPIO

In this section, we will consider a few practical methods for debugging the code driving Cortex-M GPIO pins. The General-Purpose I/O (GPIO) port of STM32 MCU is controlled through the following set of 32-bit registers listed below:

GPIOx_MODER
GPIOx_OTYPER
GPIOx_OSPEEDR
GPIOx_PUPDR
GPIOx_IDR
GPIOx_ODR
GPIOx_BSRR
GPIOx_LCKR
GPIOx_AFRL
GPIOx_AFRH

Each register from this set provides specific functions for an GPIO pin. The following examples illustrate how to debug GPIO using direct access to these registers. This gives a developer flexible control over GPIO ports and pins and allows to write fast code for I/O operations.

Example 1

Assume we want to observe how a signal on pin **PA8** of L476RGT Cortex-L4 is updated, but we don't want o connect some extra circuits such as a LED network or voltmeter to this pin. One possible method to do that is to read the corresponding GPIO input data register (GPIOA_IDR).
To illustrate this method, let's create a new STM32 Project in STM32CubeIDE with default settings and configure pin **PA8** as digital output (**Fig.78**).

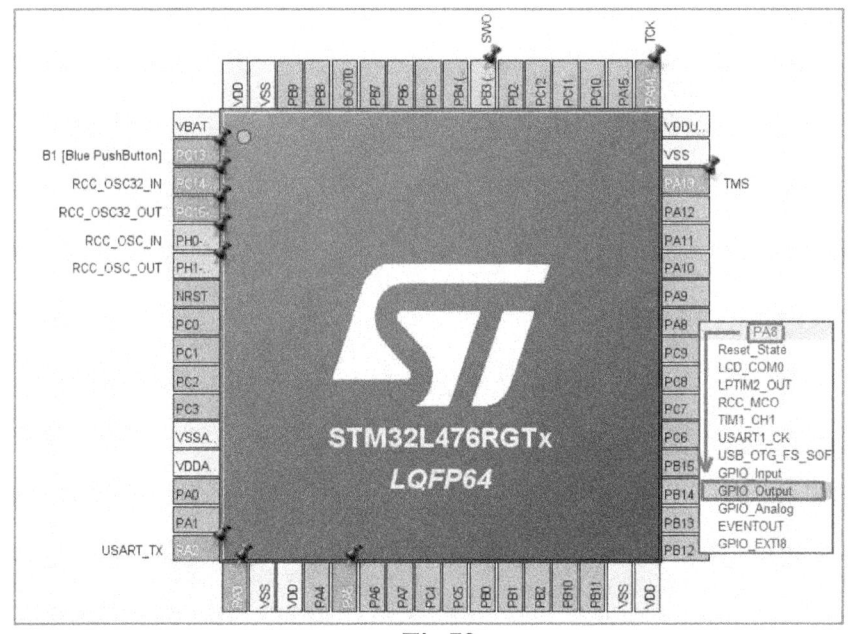

Fig.78

After the project is built without error, start the debugging session and open the **SFR** window (**Fig.79**).

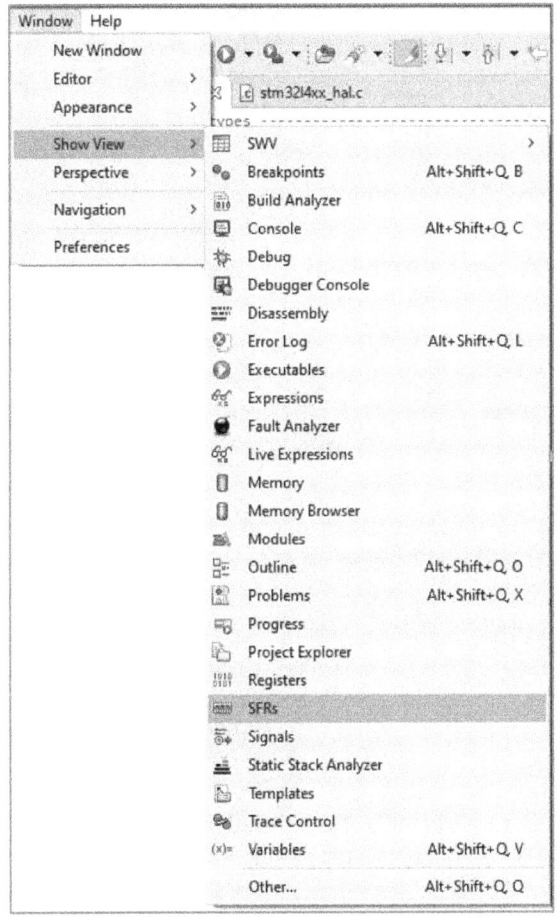

Fig.79

Then in the **SFR** window, select **GPIOA** → **ODR** → **ODR8** (**Fig.80**).

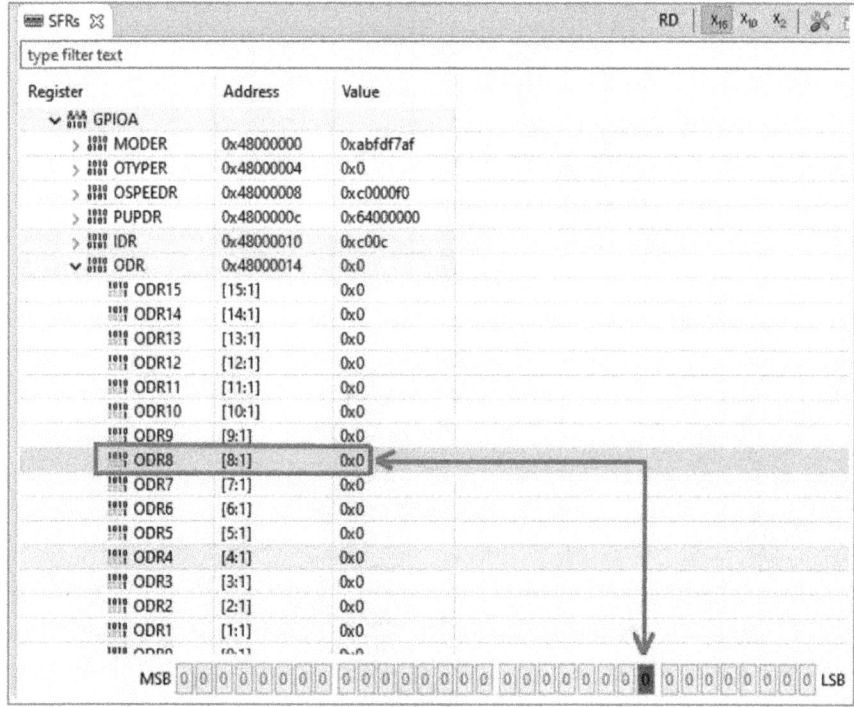

Register	Address	Value
∨ GPIOA		
> MODER	0x48000000	0xabfdf7af
> OTYPER	0x48000004	0x0
> OSPEEDR	0x48000008	0xc0000f0
> PUPDR	0x4800000c	0x64000000
> IDR	0x48000010	0xc00c
∨ ODR	0x48000014	0x0
ODR15	[15:1]	0x0
ODR14	[14:1]	0x0
ODR13	[13:1]	0x0
ODR12	[12:1]	0x0
ODR11	[11:1]	0x0
ODR10	[10:1]	0x0
ODR9	[9:1]	0x0
ODR8	[8:1]	0x0
ODR7	[7:1]	0x0
ODR6	[6:1]	0x0
ODR5	[5:1]	0x0
ODR4	[4:1]	0x0
ODR3	[3:1]	0x0
ODR2	[2:1]	0x0
ODR1	[1:1]	0x0

Fig.80

The value read from bit IDR8 (register GPIO_IDR) will be the same as that just written into bit ODR8. This is easily to explain - bit IDR8 bit reflects the state of the latch of bit ODR8 (you can find out more information on this topic in the STM32 datasheets). This is true for all GPIO pins configured as digital outputs.

The **SFR** window in **Fig.81** illustrates the case when 0x1 is written into bit ODR8.

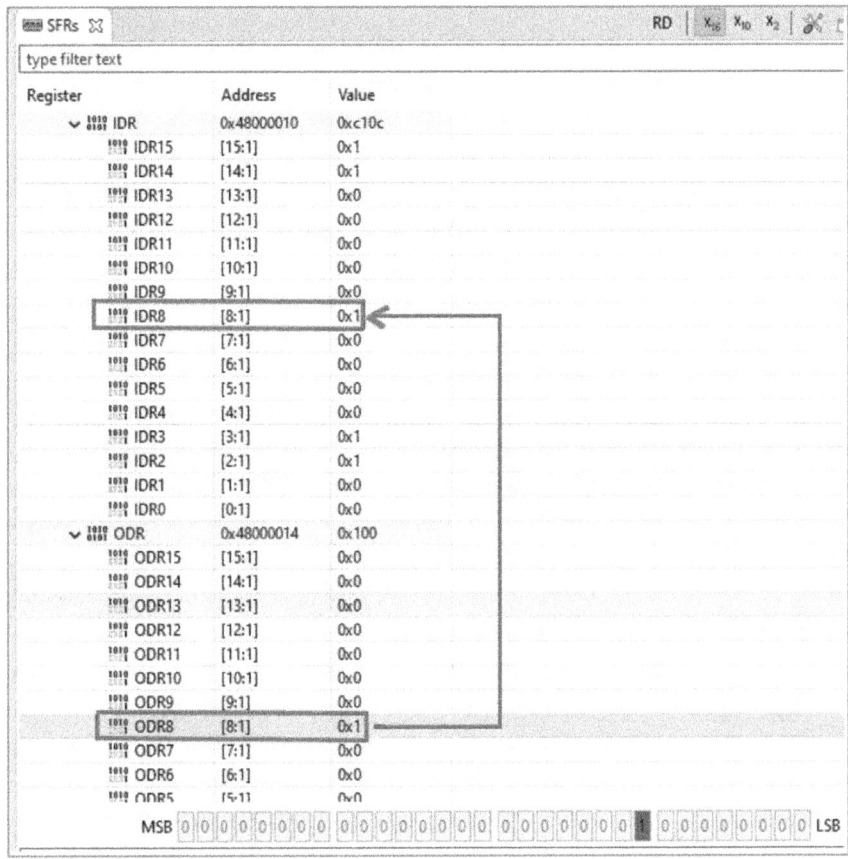

Register	Address	Value
∨ IDR	0x48000010	0xc10c
IDR15	[15:1]	0x1
IDR14	[14:1]	0x1
IDR13	[13:1]	0x0
IDR12	[12:1]	0x0
IDR11	[11:1]	0x0
IDR10	[10:1]	0x0
IDR9	[9:1]	0x0
IDR8	[8:1]	0x1
IDR7	[7:1]	0x0
IDR6	[6:1]	0x0
IDR5	[5:1]	0x0
IDR4	[4:1]	0x0
IDR3	[3:1]	0x1
IDR2	[2:1]	0x1
IDR1	[1:1]	0x0
IDR0	[0:1]	0x0
∨ ODR	0x48000014	0x100
ODR15	[15:1]	0x0
ODR14	[14:1]	0x0
ODR13	[13:1]	0x0
ODR12	[12:1]	0x0
ODR11	[11:1]	0x0
ODR10	[10:1]	0x0
ODR9	[9:1]	0x0
ODR8	[8:1]	0x1
ODR7	[7:1]	0x0
ODR6	[6:1]	0x0
ODR5	[5:1]	0x0

Fig.81

Example 2

This example shows how to display the state of digital output in the **SWV Data Trace Timeline Graph** window while debugging code.
Let's create a new STM32 Project and configure pin **PA8** as digital output. Then modify the source code of the **main()** function by inserting a few lines of code (shown in bold in **Listing 53**).

Listing 53.

#include "main.h"

uint8_t pinState;

/* Private variables ---*/
UART_HandleTypeDef huart2;

/* Private function prototypes ---*/
void SystemClock_Config(void);
static void MX_GPIO_Init(void);
static void MX_USART2_UART_Init(void);

int main(void)
{
  /* MCU Configuration--*/

  /* Reset of all peripherals, Initializes the Flash interface and the Systick. */
  HAL_Init();

  /* Configure the system clock */
  SystemClock_Config();

  /* Initialize all configured peripherals */
  MX_GPIO_Init();
  MX_USART2_UART_Init();

  while (1)
  {
  pinState = GPIOA->IDR >> 8 & 0x1;
  HAL_Delay(50);
  }
}
. . . . . .

In this code, we will examine the variable **pinState** within a **while()** loop every 50 mS. This variable will be assigned either 0x0 or 0x1 depending on the state of digital output (pin **PA8**).
If the project is built without errors, start debugging and select
SWV Data Trace Timeline Graph by clicking
Window → Show View → SWV → SWV Data Trace Timeline Graph
(**Fig.82**).

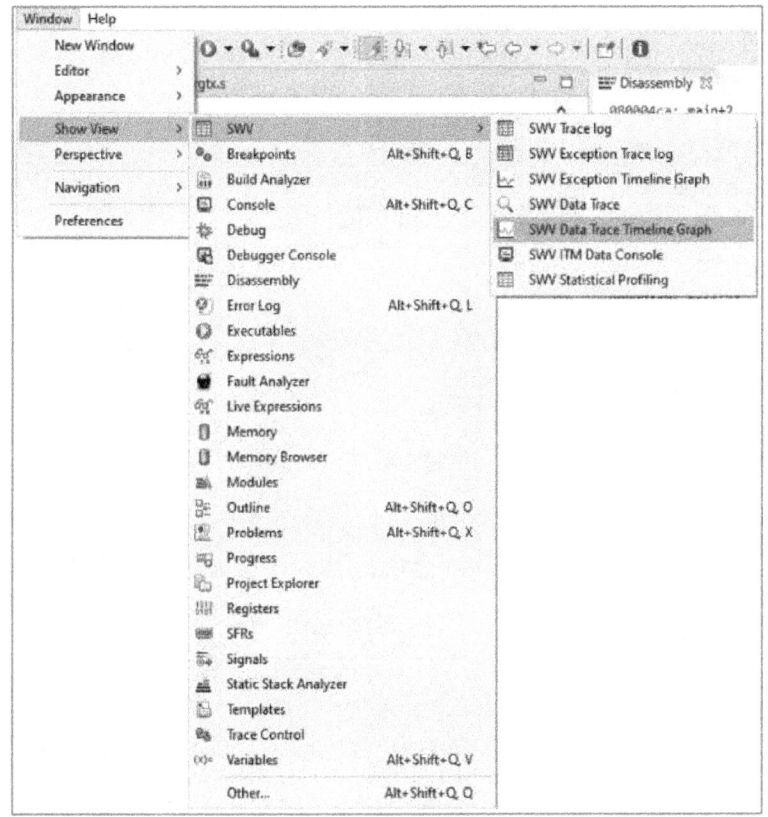

Fig.82

In the opened window (**Fig.83**), we should click **Configure trace** to set the required parameters.

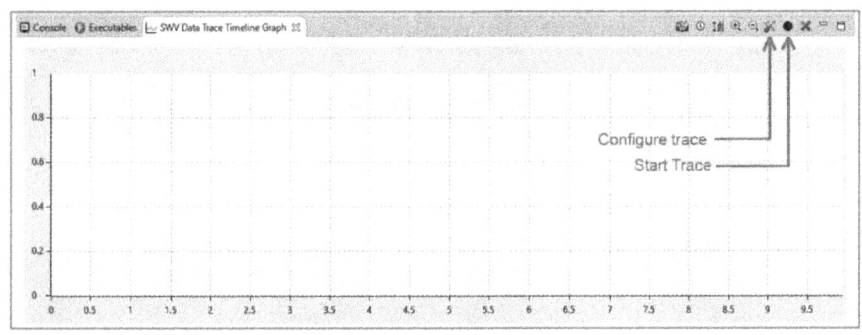

Fig.83

Then define the following parameters in the **Serial Wire Viewer** window (**Fig.84**).

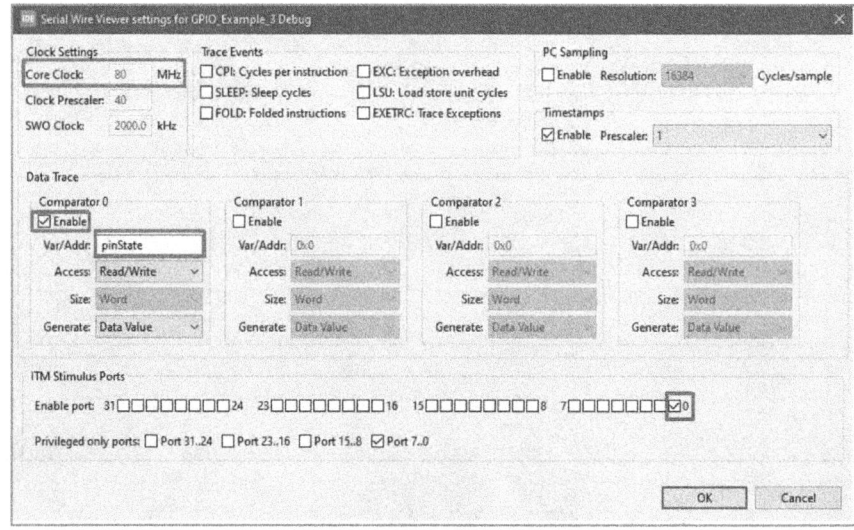

Fig.84

The **Core Clock** must be equal to the value set for your particular processor. In my case, this parameter is set to 80 MHz. Also, we need to select ITM Stimulus Port 0 to output data and define the variable **pinState** to be traced. The **Enable** field must be checked as well.

When we are done, return to the **SWV Data Trace Timeline Graph** window and click **Start Trace** (see **Fig.83**).
Then we step through the instructions until the **while()** loop is entered. At this point, open the **SFR** window (**Fig.85**) and choose bit ODR8 (=pin **PA8**).

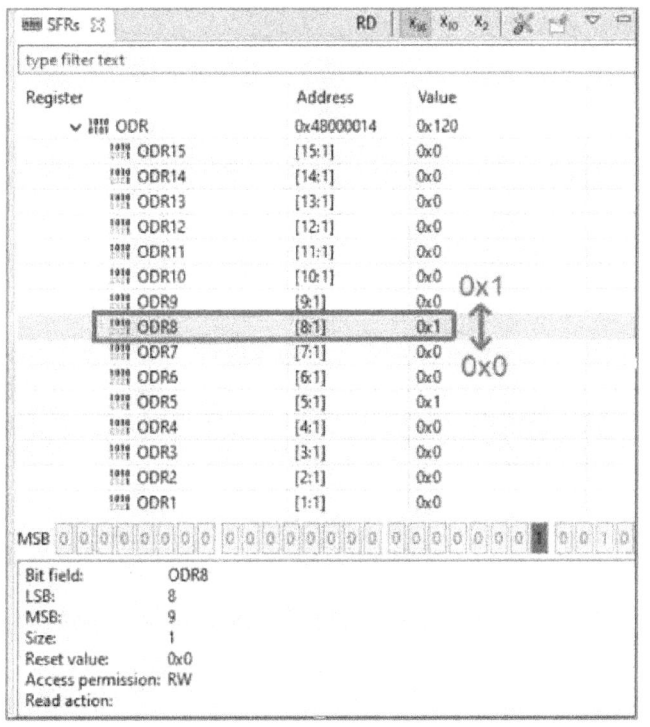

Fig.85

When bit ODR8 is updated, its state is reflected by the **statePin** variable (**Fig.86**). Therefore, through **statePin** we can see how the **PA8** output changes.

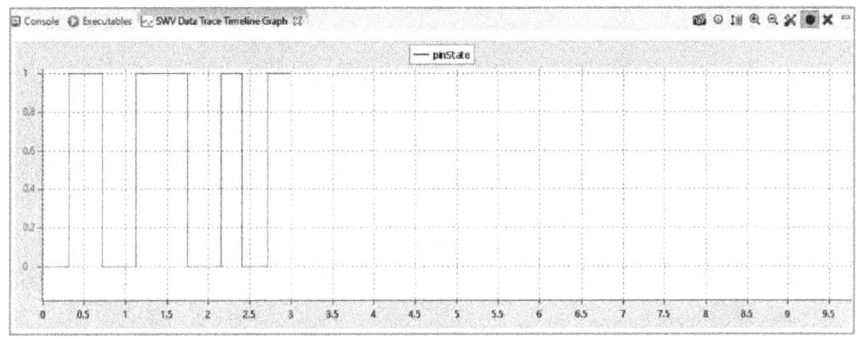

Fig.86

Example 3

Using the approach described in the previous example, we can easily trace any digital input and display data in the **SWV Data Trace Timeline Graph** window. In this example, I will use pin **PC3** that is connected to the User button on the NUCLEO-L476RG board.
After creating a new STM32 Project, pin **PC13** will be configured as digital input (**Fig.87**).

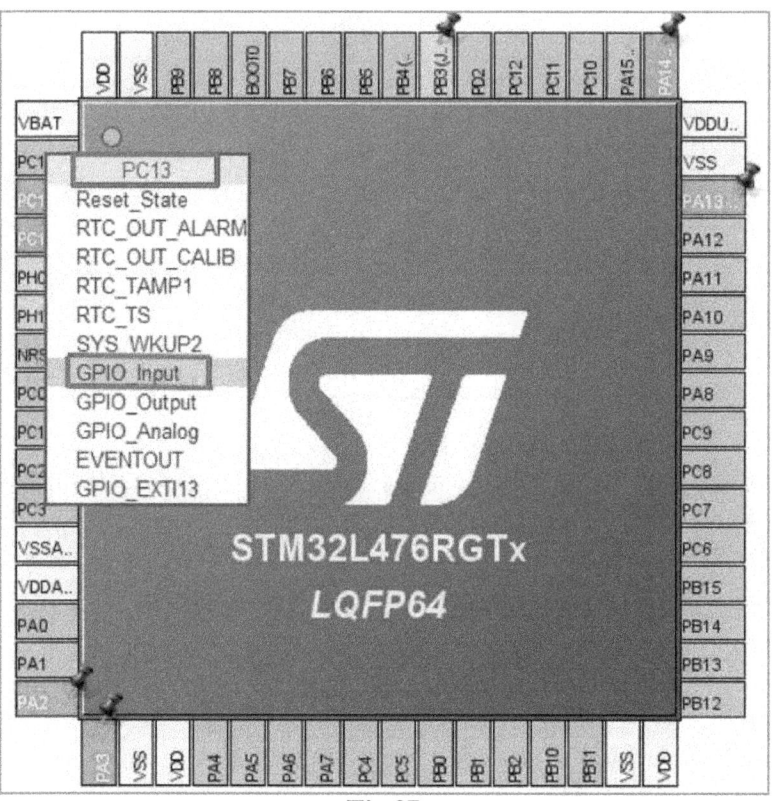

Fig.87

The settings for **PC13** are shown on the **GPIO Mode and Configuration** page (**Fig.88**).

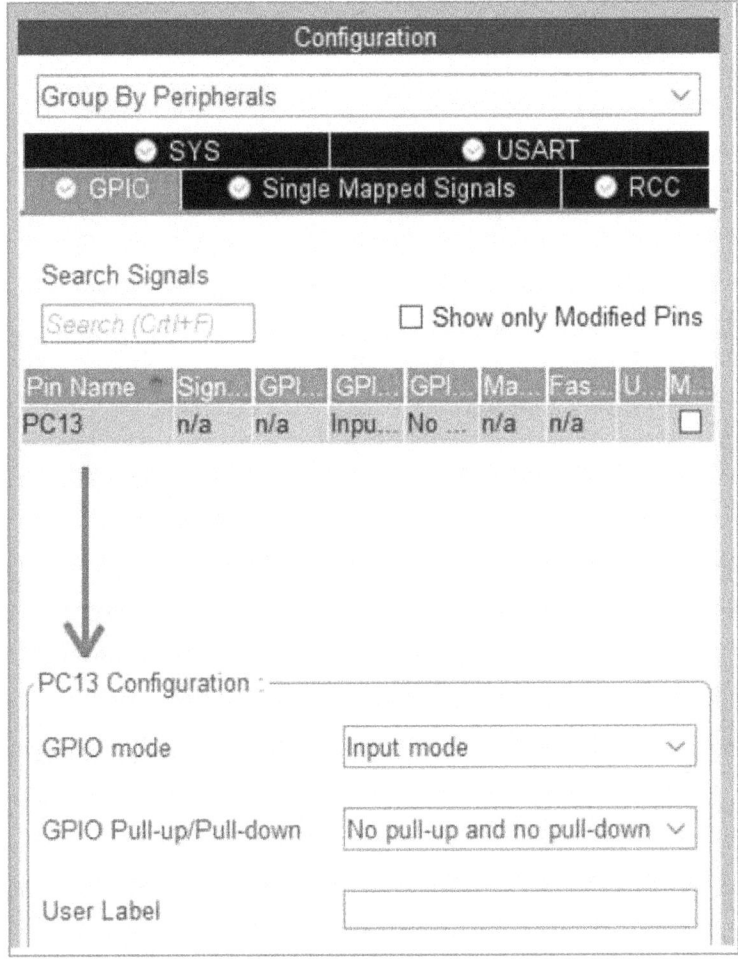

Fig.88

After STM32CubeIDE Code Generator has created the source code, we should modify the **main()** function so that to observe how the signal on digital input **PC13** is altered while the User button is pressed / released. The modified source code of **main()** is shown in **Listing 54**. The inserted lines are shown in bold.

Listing 54.

#include "main.h"

uint16_t pinState;

```
/* Private variables ---------------------------------------------------------*/
UART_HandleTypeDef huart2;

/* Private function prototypes -----------------------------------------------*/
void SystemClock_Config(void);
static void MX_GPIO_Init(void);
static void MX_USART2_UART_Init(void);

int main(void)
{
  /* MCU Configuration----------------------------------------------------------*/

  /* Reset of all peripherals, Initializes the Flash interface and the Systick. */
  HAL_Init();

  /* Configure the system clock */
  SystemClock_Config();

  /* Initialize all configured peripherals */
  MX_GPIO_Init();
  MX_USART2_UART_Init();

  while (1)
  {
    pinState = (uint16_t) GPIOC->IDR >> 13 & 0x1;
    HAL_Delay(50);
  }
}
. . . . . .
```

After the project is built without errors, launch the Debugger and select **SWV Data Trace Timeline Graph** by clicking
Window → Show View → SWV → SWV Data Trace Timeline Graph. Then configure the required parameters in the **Serial Wire Viewer** window as was already shown in **Fig.84**. After tracing has been started, we can observe how the input signal on pin **PC13** changes as the User button is pressed / released (**Fig.89**).

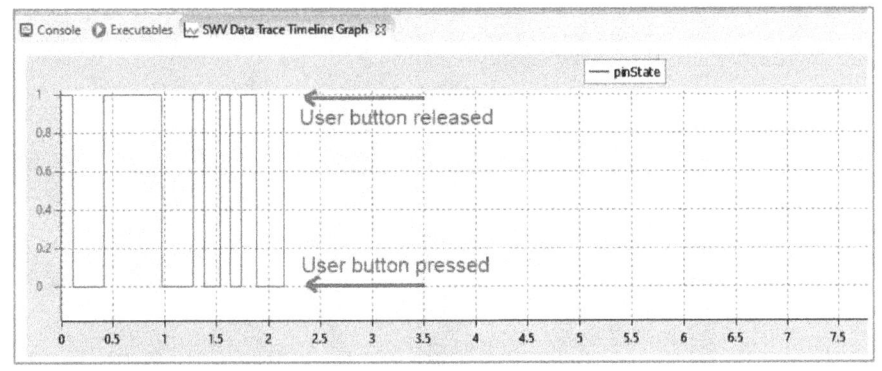

Fig.89

Example 4

This example illustrates how to handle external interrupts on GPIO input in the STM32CubeIDE.

We will process interrupts triggered by a falling edge (1-0) on pin **PC13** of the NUCLEO-L476RG board. This pin is connected to the User button, therefore it is convenient to play with the interrupt by clicking the button. Let's create a new STM32 Project where pin **PC13** will be connected to the external interrupt line 13 (**Fig.90**).

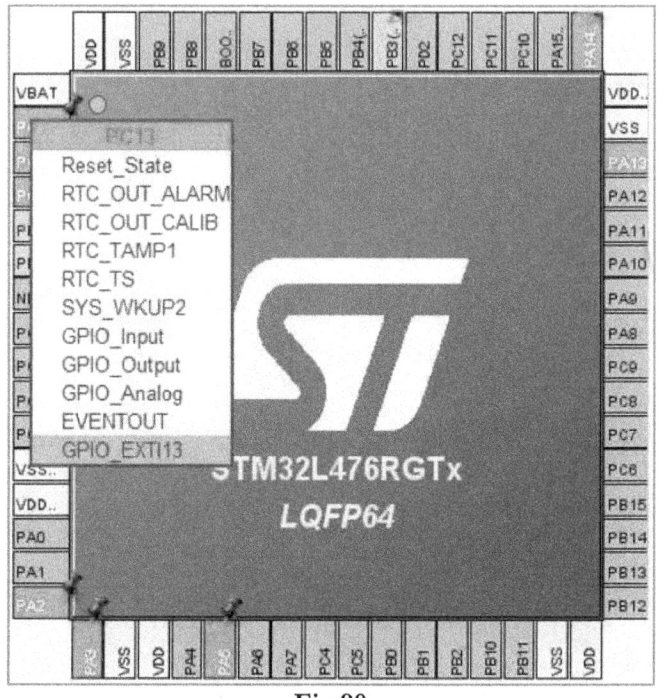

Fig.90

On the **GPIO** page of the configuration window, choose "**No pull-up and no pull-down**" and
"**External Interrupt Mode with Falling edge trigger detection**" (Fig.91).

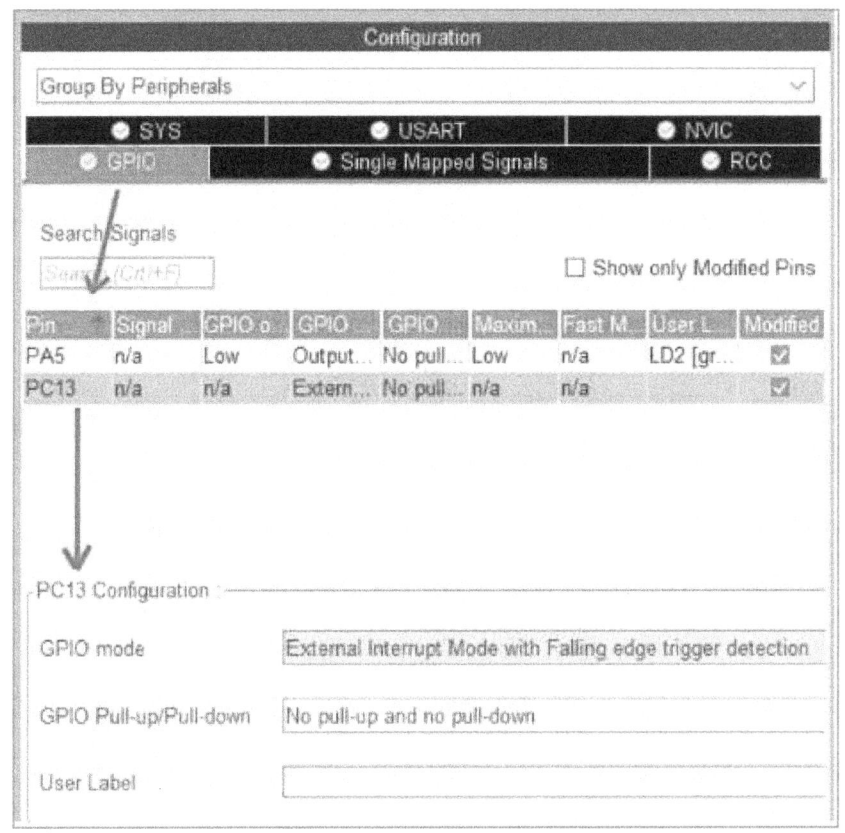

Fig.91

We also need to enable the interrupt line (=13) in the NVIC Interrupt Controller (**Fig.92**).

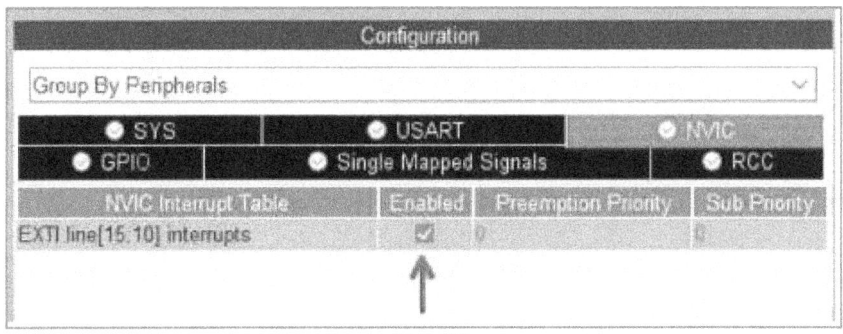

Fig.92

After the Project Wizard has finished its job, let's modify the source code of the **main()** function (file **main.c**) and **EXTI15_10_IRQHandler** Interrupt Handler (file **stm32l4xx_it.c**).

For illustrative purposes, assume that the **EXTI15_10_IRQHandler()** when invoked increments some counter by 1 until it reaches 10, then clears this counter and repeats the operation from 0. Also assume that the on-board LED (pin **PA5**, in my case) will blink each time the interrupt is triggered.

This algorithm is implemented in the source code inserted into **EXTI15_10_IRQHandler** (**Listing 55**). The inserted lines are shown in bold.

Listing 55.

```
void EXTI15_10_IRQHandler(void)
{
  /* USER CODE BEGIN EXTI15_10_IRQn 0 */

  /* USER CODE END EXTI15_10_IRQn 0 */
  HAL_GPIO_EXTI_IRQHandler(GPIO_PIN_13);
  /* USER CODE BEGIN EXTI15_10_IRQn 1 */

  HAL_GPIO_TogglePin(GPIOA, GPIO_PIN_5);
  del = 1000000;
  while (del-- != 0);
  if (cnt++ > 10) cnt = 0;

  /* USER CODE END EXTI15_10_IRQn 1 */
}
```

In this code, function **HAL_GPIO_TogglePin()** toggles the LED connected to pin **PA5**. The sequence

del = 1000000;
while (del-- != 0);

provides some delay (variable **del**) to debounce the input signal. The **cnt** variable is incremented by 1 until it reaches 10, then its value is cleared and incrementing repeats from 0.

We also need to declare both variables **del** and **cnt** as **volatile** at the beginning of the source code in **stm32l4xx_it.c** (**Listing 56**).

Listing 56.

```
/* Includes ----------------------------------------------------------*/
#include "main.h"
#include "stm32l4xx_it.h"
volatile uint32_t cnt = 0;
volatile uint32_t del;
```

In the **main()** function, we insert a couple of lines (shown in bold) before a **while(1)** loop (**Listing 57**).

Listing 57.

```
. . . . . . .
HAL_Delay(20000);
__asm("BKPT\n");
  while (1)
  {
    /* USER CODE END WHILE */

    /* USER CODE BEGIN 3 */
  }
  /* USER CODE END 3 */
}
. . . . . . .
```

After the project is built without errors, start a debugging session. Let's view how the variable **cnt** changes as the interrupt is triggered. To do that, we will use the **SWV Data Trace Timeline Graph** window, then configure the required parameters in the **Serial Wire Viewer** window to trace variable **cnt** (**Fig.93**).

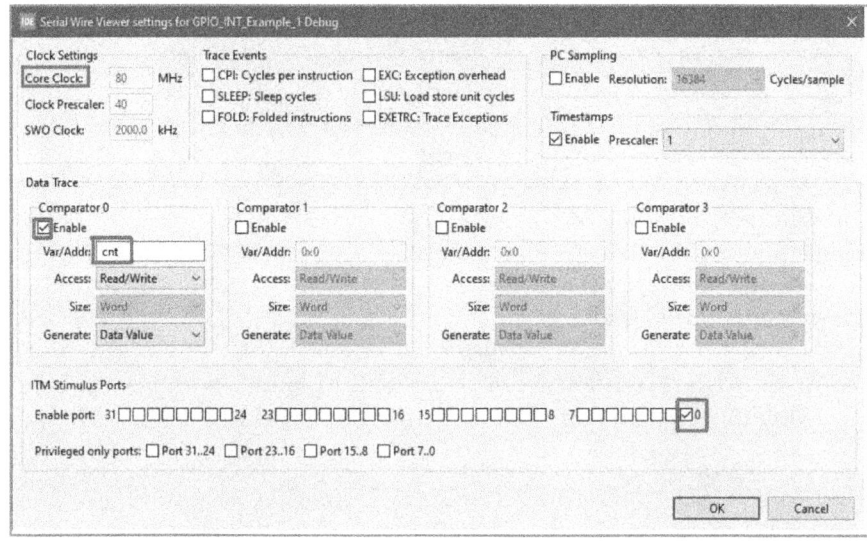

Fig.93

Then we will step through the instructions and observe how the **cnt** variable changes while the User button (pin **PC13**) is pressed (1-0, falling edge). The **SWV Data Trace Timeline Graph** window for this case is shown in **Fig.94**.

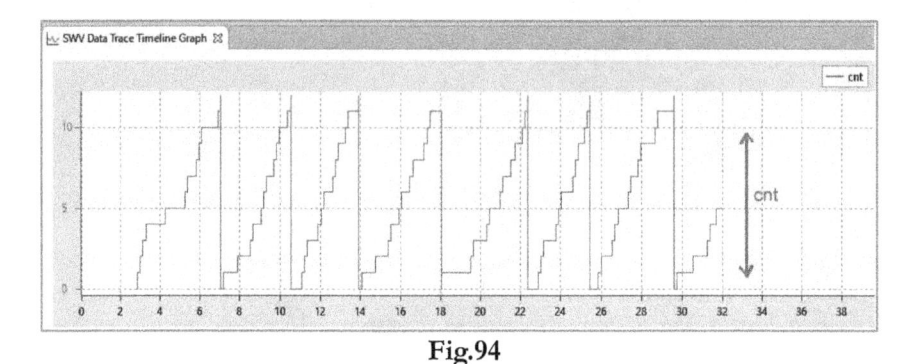

Fig.94

Example 5

This example illustrates how to debug external interrupts on some GPIO input without connecting a signal source to the GPIO pin.

Let's create a new STM32 Project and configure some GPIO pin to capture interrupts on the falling edge of an input signal. When an interrupt is triggered, the Interrupt Handler code will toggle the on-board LED. In my case, to capture an interrupt event I will use pin **PA8** on the NUCLEO-L476RG board - this pin isn't connected to any external signal source. The on-board LED is connected to pin **PA5** that is configured as digital output by default.

The configuration settings for **PA8** is shown in **Fig.95 - Fig.97**.

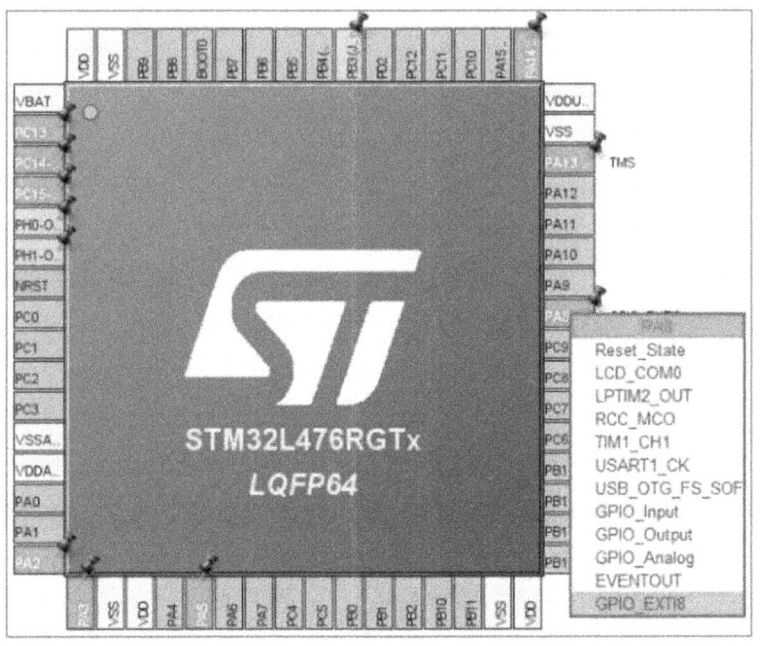

Fig.95

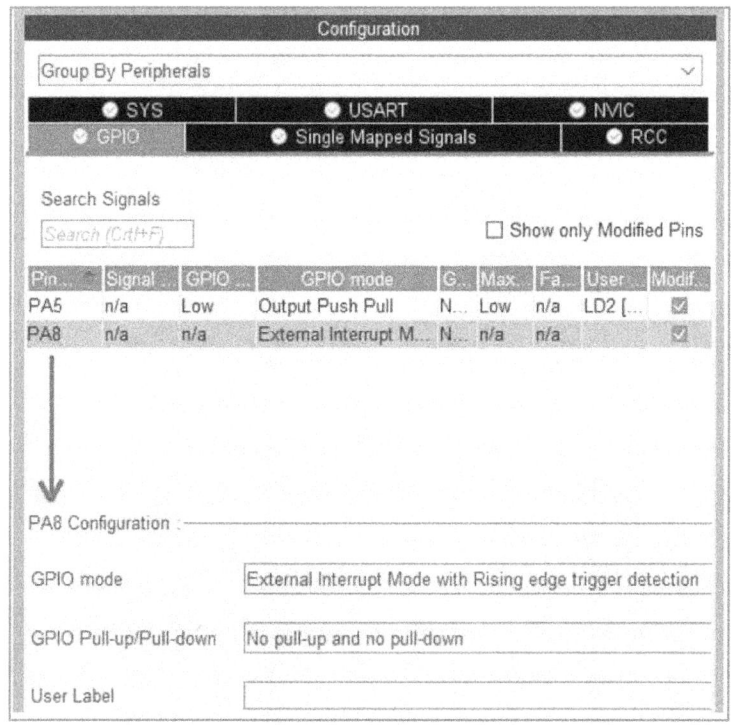

Fig.96

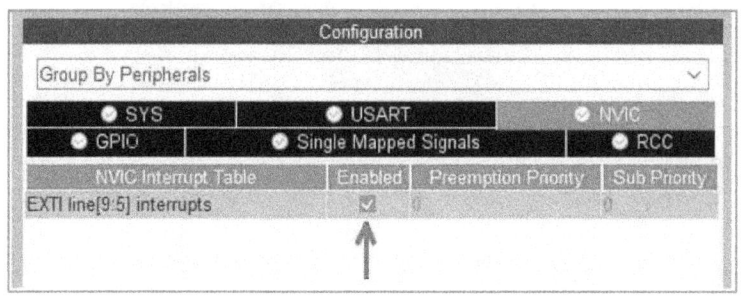

Fig.97

After the source code for this project is generated, let's modify the **main()** function (file **main.c**) and Interrupt Handler **EXTI9_5_IRQHandler()** (file **stm32l4xx_it.c**).
The **EXTI9_5_IRQHandler()** source code will then look like the following (**Listing 58**).

Listing 58.

```
void EXTI9_5_IRQHandler(void)
{
  /* USER CODE BEGIN EXTI9_5_IRQn 0 */

  /* USER CODE END EXTI9_5_IRQn 0 */
  HAL_GPIO_EXTI_IRQHandler(GPIO_PIN_8);
  /* USER CODE BEGIN EXTI9_5_IRQn 1 */

  HAL_GPIO_TogglePin(GPIOA, GPIO_PIN_5);

  /* USER CODE END EXTI9_5_IRQn 1 */
}
```

In this code, we inserted the **HAL_GPIO_TOgglePin()** statement to drive the on-board LED ON/OFF.
In the **main()** function, we insert the **HAL_Delay()** function into the **while (1)** loop (**Listing 59**).

Listing 59.

```
. . . . . . .
while (1)
  {
    /* USER CODE END WHILE */
    HAL_Delay(50000);
    /* USER CODE BEGIN 3 */
  }
. . . . . . .
```

In order to trigger some external interrupt without feeding the actual signal to digital input, we can set the corresponding bit in the Software Interrupt Event register 1 (EXTI_SWIER1). Since we use pin **PA8**, we need to set bit SWI8 (**Fig.98**) in this register to trigger an interrupt.

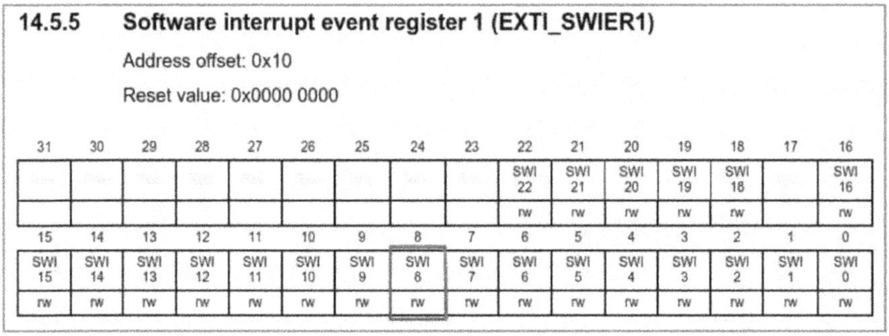

14.5.5 Software interrupt event register 1 (EXTI_SWIER1)

Address offset: 0x10

Reset value: 0x0000 0000

31	30	29	28	27	26	25	24	23	22	21	20	19	18	17	16
Res.	Res.	Res.	Res.	Res.	Res.	Res.	Res.	Res.	SWI 22	SWI 21	SWI 20	SWI 19	SWI 18	Res.	SWI 16
									rw	rw	rw	rw	rw		rw

15	14	13	12	11	10	9	8	7	6	5	4	3	2	1	0
SWI 15	SWI 14	SWI 13	SWI 12	SWI 11	SWI 10	SWI 9	SWI 8	SWI 7	SWI 6	SWI 5	SWI 4	SWI 3	SWI 2	SWI 1	SWI 0
rw	rw	rw	rw	rw	rw	rw	rw	rw	rw	rw	rw	rw	rw	rw	rw

Fig.98

After the project is built without errors, launch the Debugger. When the **HAL_Delay()** function within the **while(1)** loop begins to execute, open the **SFR** window and repeatedly set bit SWIER8 (**Fig.99**).

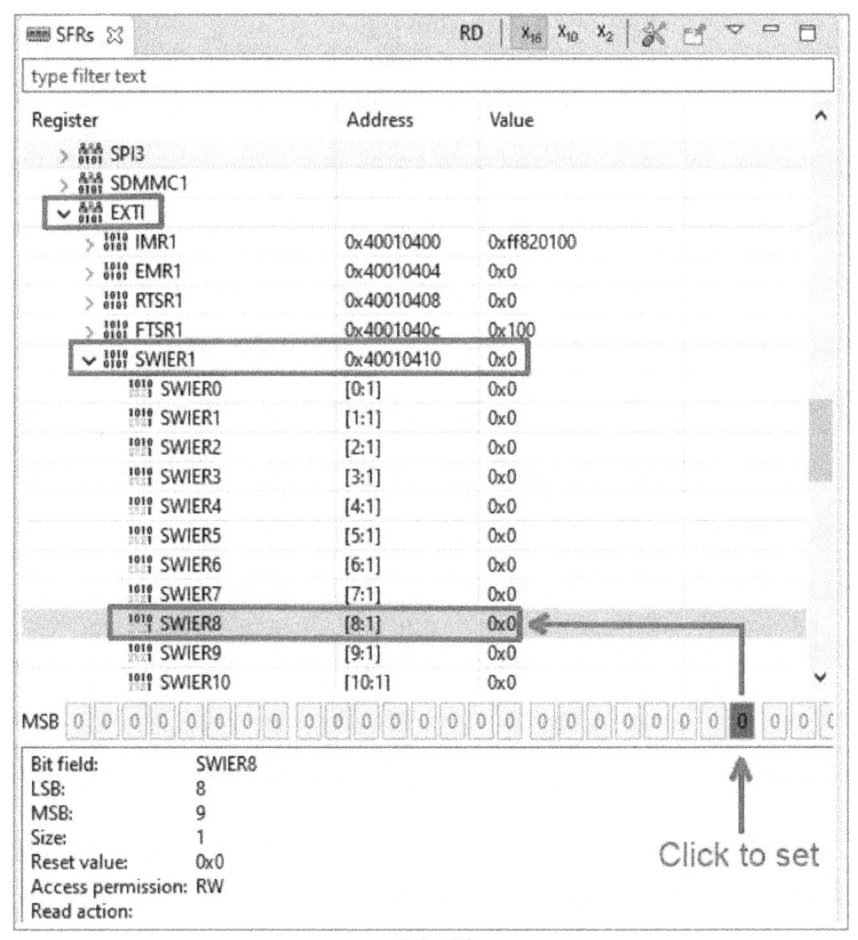

Fig.99

Each time we set bit SWIER8, the interrupt on pin **PA8** is raised and the Interrupt Handler code toggles pin **PA5** (LED). **Note** that bit SWIER8 is cleared by software when the interrupt is being processed.

Example 6

Each external interrupt can be enabled / disabled by setting /clearing the corresponding bit in the Interrupt Mask register 1 (EXTI_IMR1). This is

useful, for example, when we need to temporary disable some interrupt to examine code / data. Then we can enable the interrupt again.
The following example illustrates how to handle the external interrupt on pin **PA8** through bit 8 in EXTI_IMR1. We will use the code from the previous example with the modifications in a **while (1)** loop of the **main()** function (**Listing 60**).

Listing 60.

```
. . . . . . .
while (1)
  {
   EXTI->SWIER1 |= 0x1<<8;
   HAL_Delay(2000);
  }
. . . . . . .
```

After the project is built without errors, launch the Debugger. By stepping through the instructions within a **while(1)** loop we will raise the interrupt on **PA8** thus causing pin **PA5** to change its state. Repeating the sequence within the **while(1)** loop, we will drive the on-board LED ON/OFF. This will continue until we clear bit MR8 in the Interrupt mask register 1 (EXTI_IMR1) in the **SFR** window (**Fig.100**).

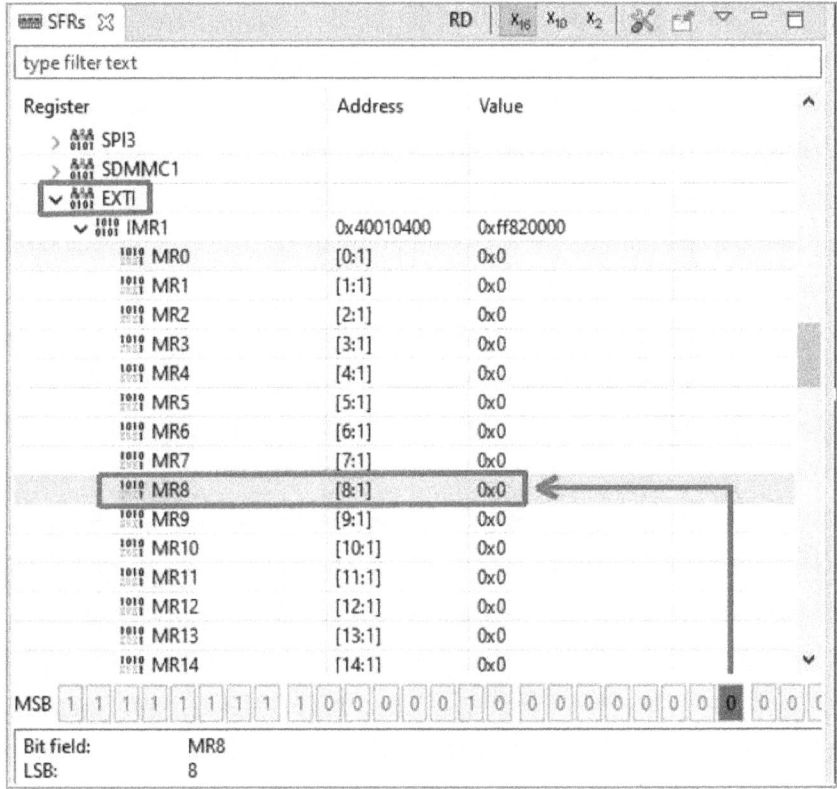

Fig.100

If bit MR8 is assigned 0x0, the interrupt is disabled. In this case, even when bit SWIER8 is set, the interrupt will not be triggered. Overwise, when MR8 is set (= 0x1) again, the interrupt is enabled and we will be capable of raising the interrupt through bit SWIER8.
Note that when we enable the interrupt again (MR8 = 0x1), we also need to clear bit SWIER8 before stepping through the code.

Debugging Timers

Programming timers in STM32CubeIDE is relatively simple task because the Code Generator makes all job for us. Debugging timers may be a more complicated task because we need to understand how to operate with data in the memory-mapped registers belonging to each timer.

The following sections illustrate a few practical methods for debugging timers.

Configuring and debugging PWM

This example illustrates how to configure and debug PWM based upon Timer 1 (TIM1). As usual, we need to create a new STM32 Project with peripherals configured with their default mode. Since we use TIM1, we should select the suitable clocking frequency for this device.
In my case, I consult the **Clock Configuration** window that looks like the following (**Fig.101**).

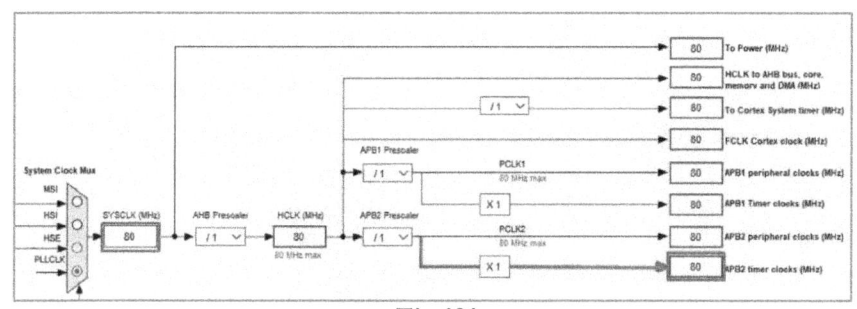

Fig.101

It is seen that the Project Wizard set the SYSCLK and APB2 bus frequency to 80 MHz by default. Since Timer 1 is attached to APB2, its clock frequency will also be 80 MHz that is suitable for our project.

To configure Timer 1, let's move to the **Pin & Configuration** window and choose TIM1. Then in the **TIM Mode and Configuration** window choose Channel 1→**PWM Generation CH1** (**Fig.102**).

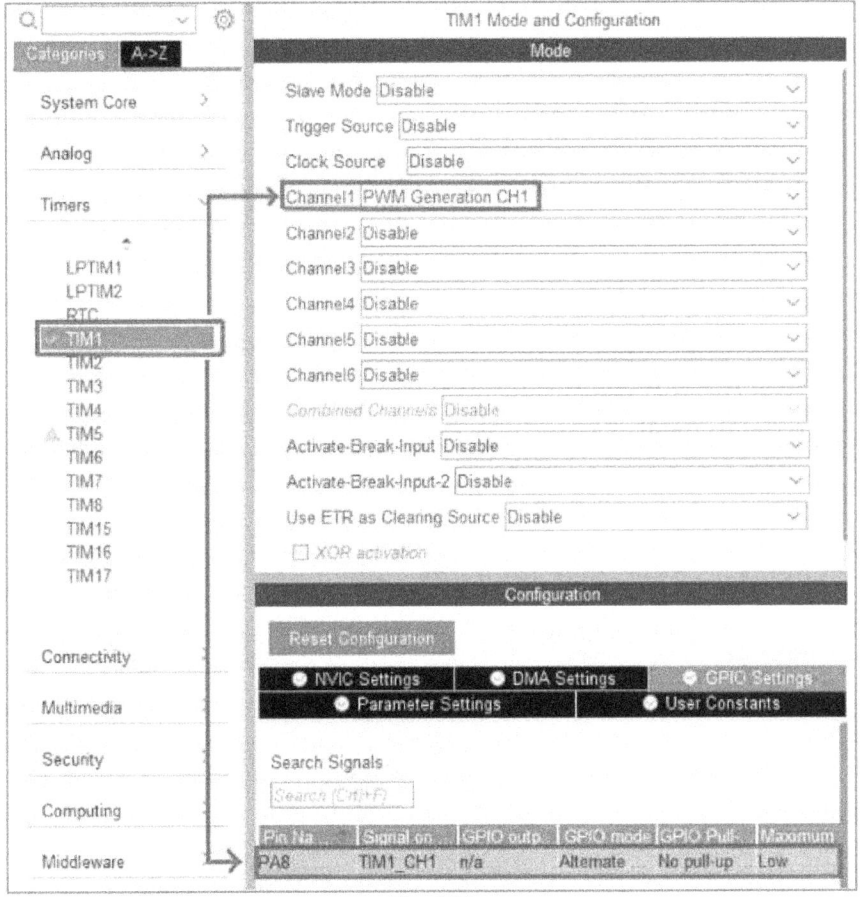

Fig.102

In this case, the PWM signal will be generated on **Channel 1** with output provided through pin **PA8** of a microcontroller.
Save the configuration and update the code. The rest of parameters for TIM1 will be set by modifying the source code of the **MX_TIM1_Init()** function placed in the **main()** function.
Assume that the PWM signal has a base frequency of 1000 Hz (Period = 1 mS). To set such frequency, modify two lines within the **MX_TIM1_Init()** function as is shown below:

htim1.Init.Prescaler = 800;
htim1.Init.Period = 100;

Also assume that the pulse width (duty cycle) of the output signal will be 70% (Period x 0.7 = 70). To configure this parameter, let's modify the following line as is shown below:

sConfigOC.Pulse = 70;

When we are done, start PWM by inserting the following statement at the end of the function:

HAL_TIM_PWM_Start(&htim1, TIM_CHANNEL_1);

Save the changes and build the project.
Let's look at how to configure the parameters of PWM while debugging code. In the Debugger, we can change either the base frequency (=1000 Hz) or pulse width (duty cycle) using TIM1 registers.
While TIM1 is enabled, the PWM signal on pin **PA8** captured by a logic analyzer looks like the following (**Fig.103**).

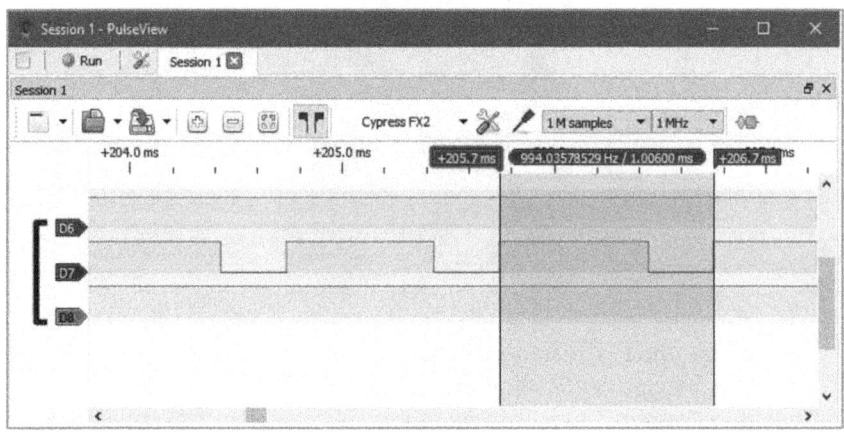

Fig.103

We can change the duty cycle of PWM "on the fly" by writing the suitable value into the TIM1 capture/compare register 1 (TIM1_CCR1). This register contains the value of a pulse width of Channel 1. The required value can be written into this register through the **SFR** window (**Fig.104)**.
In this particular case, the pulse width (duty cycle) is set to 10%.

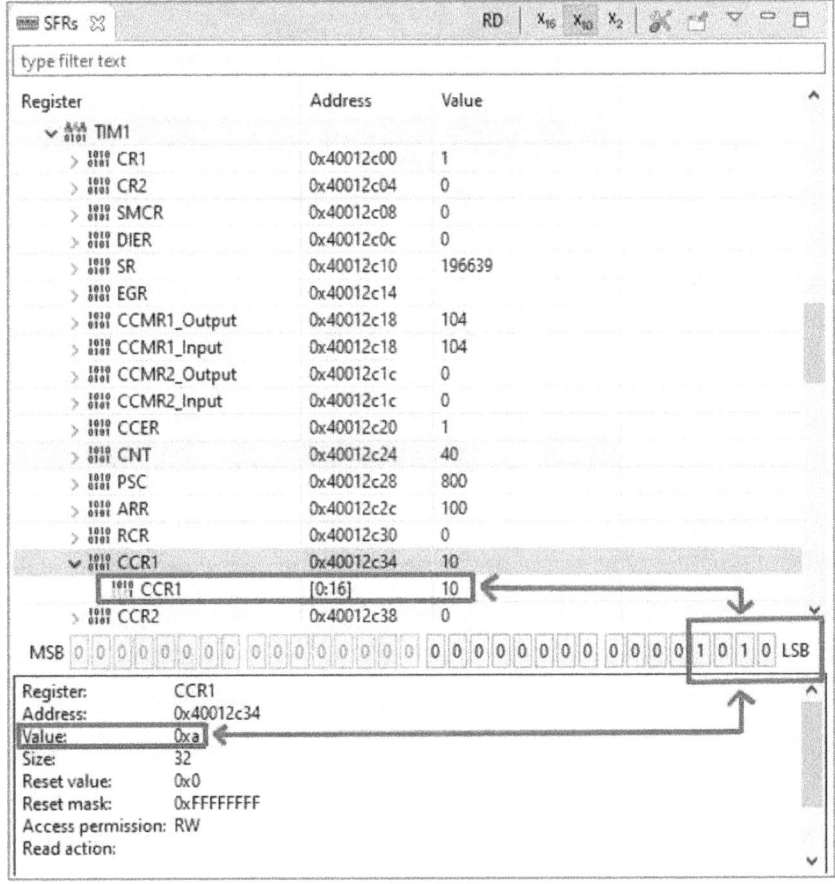

Fig.104

This immediately changes the pulse width of the signal as is illustrated in **Fig.105**.

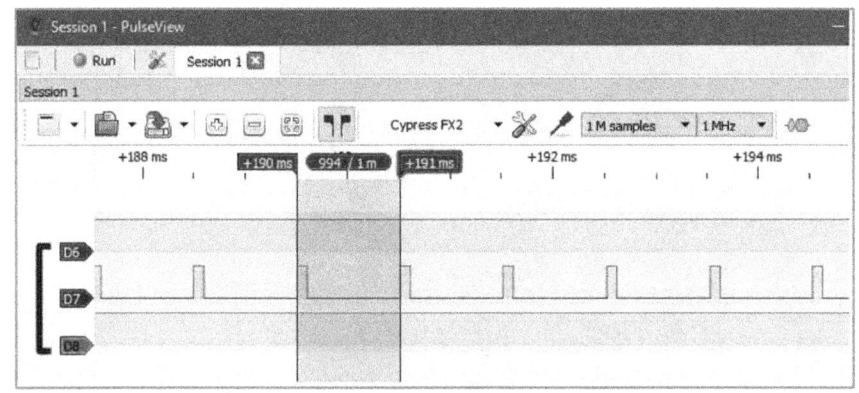

Fig.105

To change the base frequency of a PWM signal, we can write the new value into the TIM1 prescaler (TIM1_PSC) and / or TIM1 auto-reload register (TIM1_ARR). **Note** that when we change TIM_ARR, we should also recalculate the value placed in the capture/compare register TIM1_CCR1 in order to keep the duty cycle unchanged.

The following diagram (**Fig.106**) illustrates how to set the base PWM frequency on the 1 Channel 1 output equal to 2000 Hz. Here we change only the value of the TIM1 prescaler (TIM1_PSC = 400) that keeps the duty cycle (=10%) unchanged.

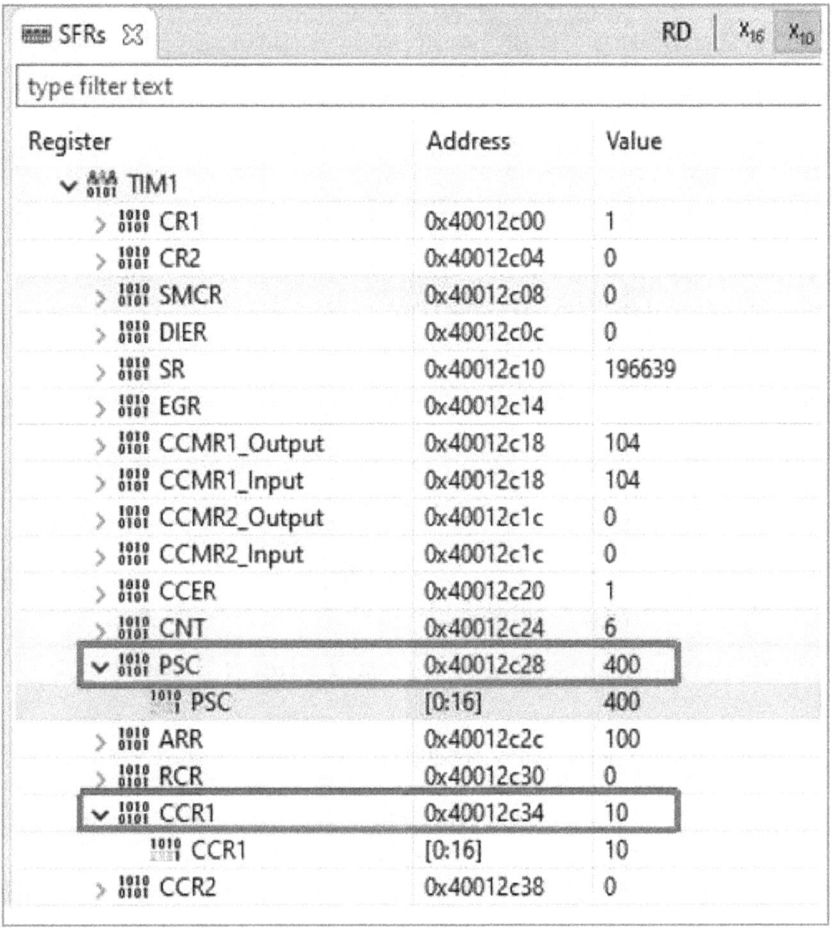

Register	Address	Value
∨ TIM1		
> CR1	0x40012c00	1
> CR2	0x40012c04	0
> SMCR	0x40012c08	0
> DIER	0x40012c0c	0
> SR	0x40012c10	196639
> EGR	0x40012c14	
> CCMR1_Output	0x40012c18	104
> CCMR1_Input	0x40012c18	104
> CCMR2_Output	0x40012c1c	0
> CCMR2_Input	0x40012c1c	0
> CCER	0x40012c20	1
> CNT	0x40012c24	6
∨ PSC	0x40012c28	400
PSC	[0:16]	400
> ARR	0x40012c2c	100
> RCR	0x40012c30	0
∨ CCR1	0x40012c34	10
CCR1	[0:16]	10
> CCR2	0x40012c38	0

Fig.106

When we need to enable / disable generating PWM, we can simply set / clear bit CEN (bit 0) in the TIM1 control register 1 (TIM1_CR1). When bit CEN is set (=0x1), the counter of TIM1 is running. When bit CEN is cleared (=0x0), the counter is stopped. The **SFR** window in **Fig.107** illustrates the case when the counter of Timer 1 is stopped.

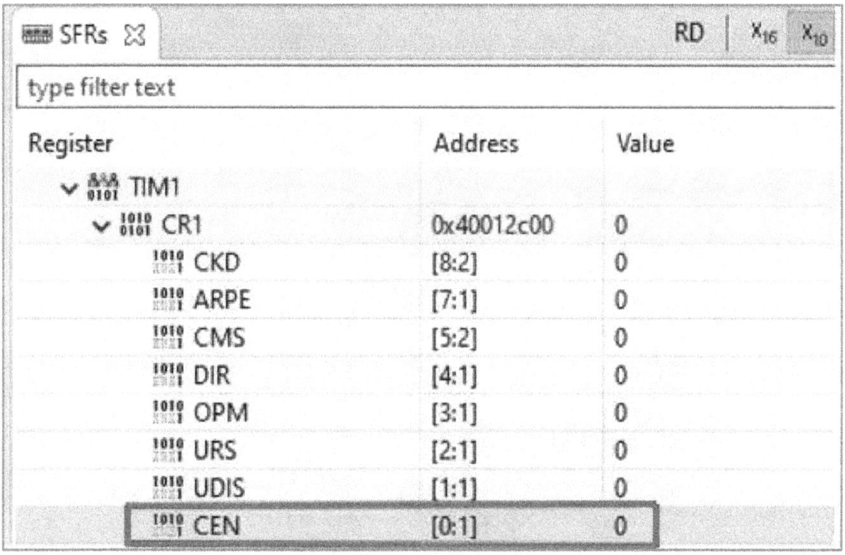

Register	Address	Value
∨ TIM1		
∨ CR1	0x40012c00	0
CKD	[8:2]	0
ARPE	[7:1]	0
CMS	[5:2]	0
DIR	[4:1]	0
OPM	[3:1]	0
URS	[2:1]	0
UDIS	[1:1]	0
CEN	**[0:1]**	**0**

Fig.107

Building a Logic Analyzer for Timers: Example 1

In this example, we will build a simple logic analyzer that will capture the PWM signal on the Channel 1 output (pin **PA8**) of TIM1. To output data, our logic analyzer will use the **SWV Data Trace Timeline Graph** window. Building the analyzer involves a few steps described below.

1. Create a new STM32 Project with default settings and generate the code that will initialize and start PWM on Channel 1 of TIM1.

2. Assume that our PWM signal will have the base frequency of 50 Hz and duty cycle = 70%. In this case, we need to modify the source code of function **MX_TIM1_Init()** as is shown in **Listing 61**.

Listing 61.

htim1.Init.Prescaler = 8000;
. . . .
htim1.Init.Period = 200; // f = 50 Hz (Period = 20 mS)
. . . .

sConfigOC.Pulse = 140;

To start PWM, we insert the following statement at the end of **MX_TIM1_Init()**:

HAL_TIM_PWM_Start(&htim1, TIM_CHANNEL_1);

3. To observe the PWM signal on pin **PA8**, we should continuously read this pin and output the result onto the **SWV Data Trace Timeline Graph**. Reading pin **PA8** can be done within function **SysTick_Handler()** (file **stm32l4xx_it.c**) that handles System Tick timer.
Let's open the **stm32l4xx_it.c** file and declare the variable **pwmOut** at the beginning of a source code (**Listing 62**).

Listing 62.

```
#include "main.h"
#include "stm32l4xx_it.h"
volatile uint32_t pwmOut;
. . . . . . .
```

Then insert the statement

pwmOut = (uint32_t)(GPIOA->IDR >> 8 & 0x1);

into the **SysTick_Handler()** as is shown in **Listing 63**.

Listing 63.

```
void SysTick_Handler(void)
{
  /* USER CODE BEGIN SysTick_IRQn 0 */

  /* USER CODE END SysTick_IRQn 0 */
  HAL_IncTick();
  /* USER CODE BEGIN SysTick_IRQn 1 */

  pwmOut = (uint32_t)(GPIOA->IDR >> 8 & 0x1);

  /* USER CODE END SysTick_IRQn 1 */
```

}

By default, the **SysTick_Handler()** handler is invoked every 1 mS - this is defined by the **SystemCoreClock** variable being set to 0x4000270F, which gives a reference time base of 1 ms with the SysTick clock set to 10 MHz (max f_{HCLK} /8 = 80 MHz / 8 = 10 MHz).

Therefore, we can output the value of **pwmOut** every 1 mS. To achieve better resolution, we can reduce this time. In this particular example, I set the reference time base to 0.4 mS (frequency = 2.5kHz) by inserting the function

HAL_SYSTICK_Config(SystemCoreClock / 2500);

into the **main()** source code as is shown in **Listing 64**.

Listing 64.

```
. . . . . . .
/* Initialize all configured peripherals */
  MX_GPIO_Init();
  MX_USART2_UART_Init();
  MX_TIM1_Init();
  /* USER CODE BEGIN 2 */

  HAL_SYSTICK_Config(SystemCoreClock / 2500);

  while (1)
  {
    HAL_Delay(20000);
  }
}
. . . . . . .
```

In this code, we also need to perform some delay (**HAL_Delay(20000)**) within a **while (1)** loop in order to start data collecting.

4. After the project is built without errors, start a debugging. session and set the parameters in **Serial Wire Viewer** window as is shown in **Fig.108**.

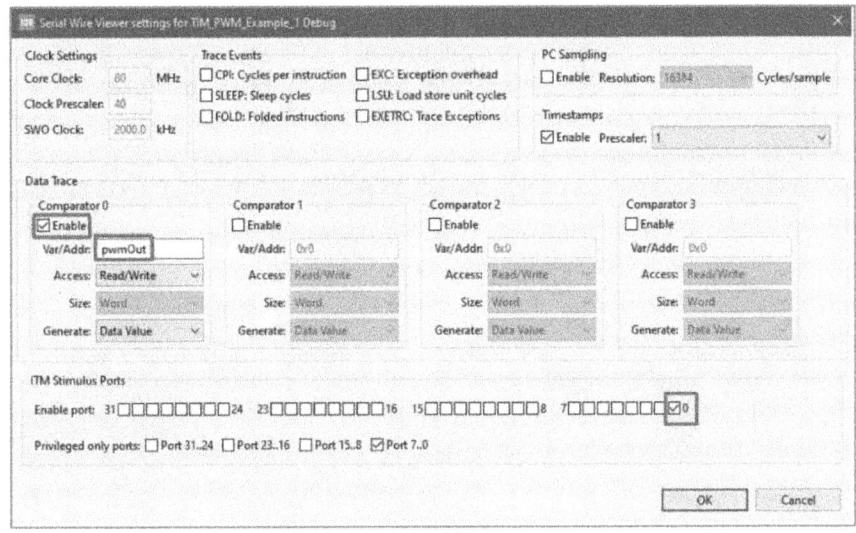

Fig.108

It is seen that we will trace the **pwmOut** variable that reflects the state of output of pin **PA8**. Click **OK** and in the **Timeline Graph** window click **"Start Trace"**. After some time passes, click **"Suspend"** to stop tracing, then use **"Zoom in"** and **"Zoom out"** to adjust the graph parameters. The output will look like the following (**Fig.109**).

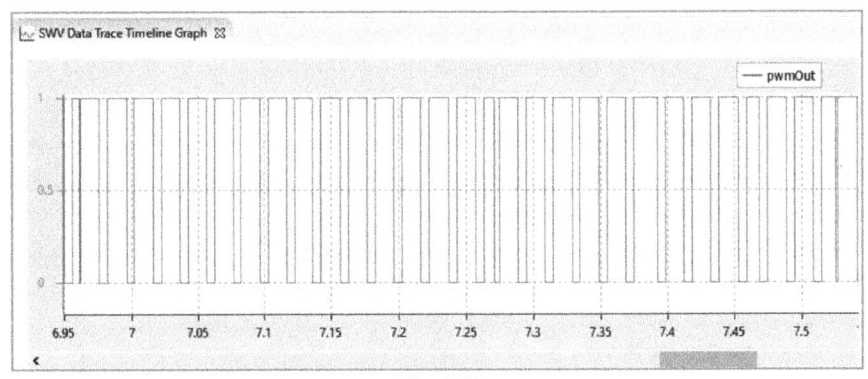

Fig.109

Building a Logic Analyzer for Timers: Example 2

One more logic analyzer can be built for tracing a counter of timers. To output data, our logic analyzer will use the **SWV Data Trace Timeline Graph** window. In this example, we will investigate the counter of Timer 1. To build a logic analyzer, we should make little modifications in the source code taken from the previous example. The modified source code of the file **stm32l4xx_it.c** now looks like the following (**Listing 65**).

Listing 65.

```
#include "main.h"
#include "stm32l4xx_it.h"
volatile uint32_t pwmOut;
volatile uint32_t cnt;
. . . . . . .

void SysTick_Handler(void)
{
  /* USER CODE BEGIN SysTick_IRQn 0 */

  /* USER CODE END SysTick_IRQn 0 */
  HAL_IncTick();
  /* USER CODE BEGIN SysTick_IRQn 1 */

  pwmOut = (uint32_t)(GPIOA->IDR >> 8 & 0x1);
  cnt = TIM1->CNT;

  /* USER CODE END SysTick_IRQn 1 */
}
. . . . . .
```

Here we defined the variable **cnt** that will store the current value of the TIM1 counter using the statement

cnt = TIM1->CNT;

After the project is built without errors, launch the Debugger and add the **cnt** variable in the **Serial Wire Viewer** (**Fig.110**) - this will allow to trace this variable in the **SWV Data Trace Timline Graph** window.

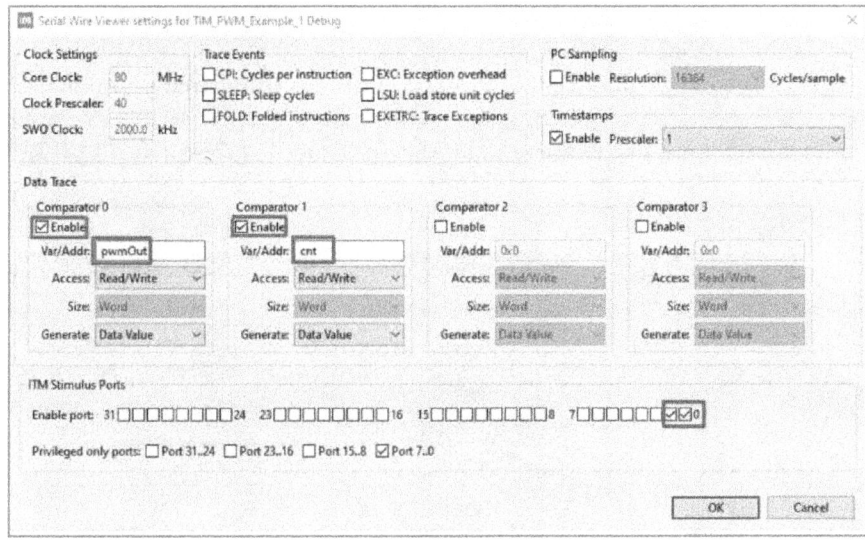

Fig.110

Then we will step through the code. When function **HAL_Delay()** within the **while (1)** loop begins to execute, the data will appear on the timeline graph. After some time has passed, suspend debugging and examine the graph. In my case, this looks like the following (**Fig.111**).

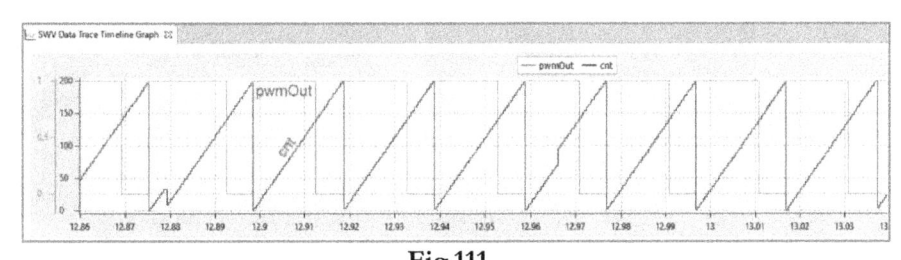

Fig.111

Building a Logic Analyzer for Timers: Example 3

The logic analyzer described in this section allows to trace counter of Timer 1 (TIM1) using the TIM1 capture compare interrupt. As in the previous examples, Timer 1 produces the PWM signal on Channel 1. To output data, our logic analyzer will use the **SWV Data Trace Timeline Graph** window.

145

Additionally, we need to enable the TIM1 capture compare interrupt and use a base frequency of a PWM signal as a reference time base while timing data in the timeline graph window.

After creating a new STM32 Project, Timer 1 is configured to produce the PWM signal with a base frequency of 100 Hz (period = 10 mS) and a duty cycle of 60%. The configuration page of Timer 1 is shown in (**Fig.112**).

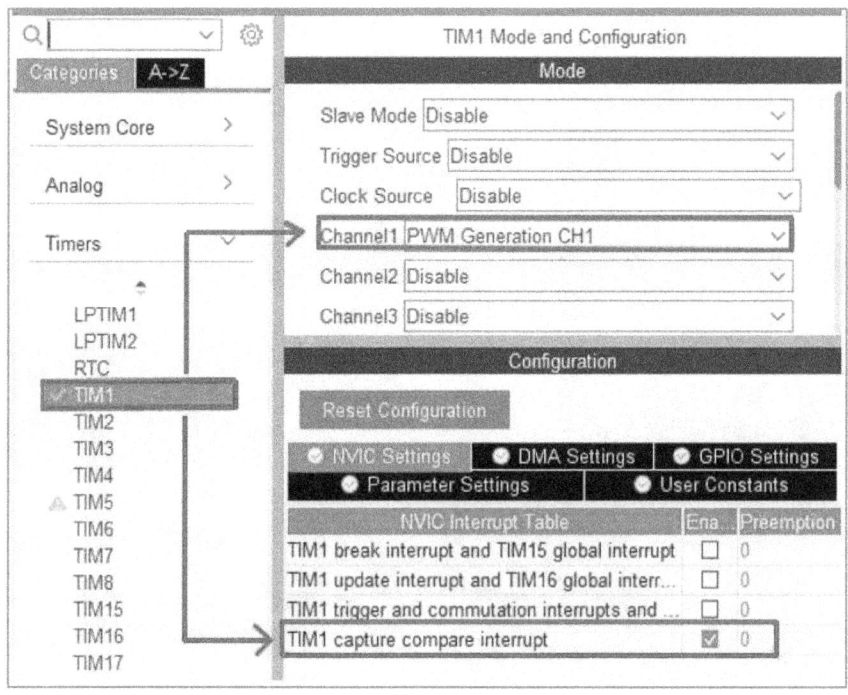

Fig.112

After the Project Wizard has finished its job, we need to modify the source code in the **main.c** and **stm32l4xx_it.c** files.

The **stm32l4xx_it.c** file now contains the source code of the capture compare Interrupt Handler **TIM1_CC_IRQHandler()**.

The modified source code of this Interrupt Handler is shown in **Listing 66**.

Listing 66.

```
void TIM1_CC_IRQHandler(void)
{
  /* USER CODE BEGIN TIM1_CC_IRQn 0 */
```

```
/* USER CODE END TIM1_CC_IRQn 0 */
HAL_TIM_IRQHandler(&htim1);
/* USER CODE BEGIN TIM1_CC_IRQn 1 */
ccFlag = (uint32_t)TIM1->CNT;
  __asm(
        "push   {r0}\n"
        "mov    r0, #20\n"
"next:\n"
        "subs   r0, r0, #1\n"
        "bgt    next\n"
        "pop    {r0}\n"
   );
  ccFlag = 0;
  /* USER CODE END TIM1_CC_IRQn 1 */
}
```

In this code, I use variable **ccFlag** to store the value of the counter. The **ccFlag** variable is defined at the beginning of a source code (**Listing 67**).

Listing 67.

```
. . . . . . .
#include "main.h"
#include "stm32l4xx_it.h"
volatile uint32_t ccFlag;
. . . . . . .
```

The optional **__asm()** code fragment within the Interrupt Handler provides a small delay before **ccFlag** is cleared.

The **HAL_Delay()** function (**Listing 68**) in the **while (1)** loop of **main()** provides some delay.

Listing 68.

```
. . . . . . .
while (1)
  {
    /* USER CODE END WHILE */
```

```
  HAL_Delay(20000);
  /* USER CODE BEGIN 3 */
}
/* USER CODE END 3 */
```
. . . .

Additionally, we modify a few lines of the source code in the **MX_TIM1_Init()** function in order to set the base PWM frequency equal to 100 Hz and the duty cycle = 60% (**Listing 69**).

Listing 69.

```
htim1.Init.Prescaler = 8000;
```
. . . .
```
htim1.Init.Period = 100; // f = 100 Hz  (T = 10 mS)
```
. . . .
```
sConfigOC.Pulse = 60;
```

Note that the above values are calculated for SYSCLK = 80 MHz. To start PWM, the following statement was inserted at the end of **MX_TIM1_Init()**:

```
HAL_TIM_PWM_Start_IT(&htim1, TIM_CHANNEL_1);
```

Save changes and build the project. If there are no errors, we can start the Debugger and then indicate the **ccFlag** variable as to be traced in the **Serial Wire Viewer** configuration window (**Fig.113**).

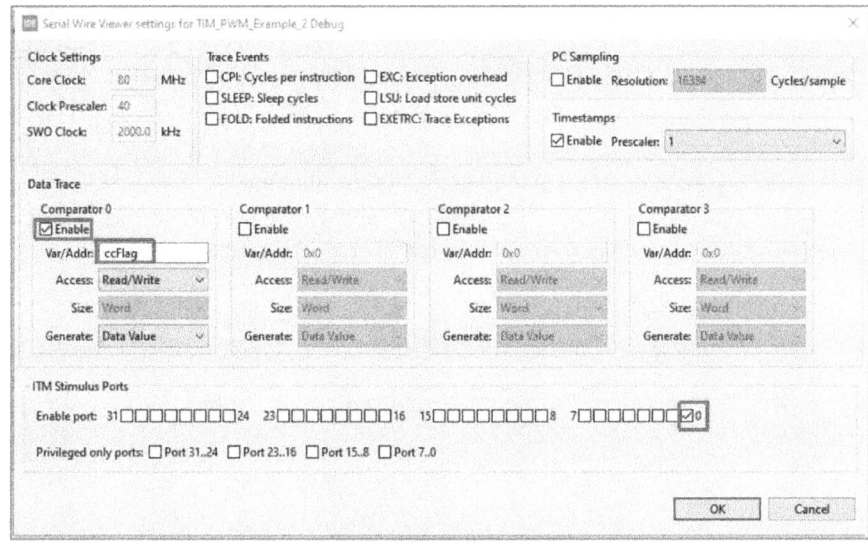

Fig.113

In debugging mode, when function **HAL_Delay()** within the **while (1)** begins to execute, the data (values of **ccFlag**) appears in the **SWV Data Trace Timeline Graph** window. After some time passed, suspend debugging and adjust the graph for better viewing and examining data as is shown in **Fig.114**.

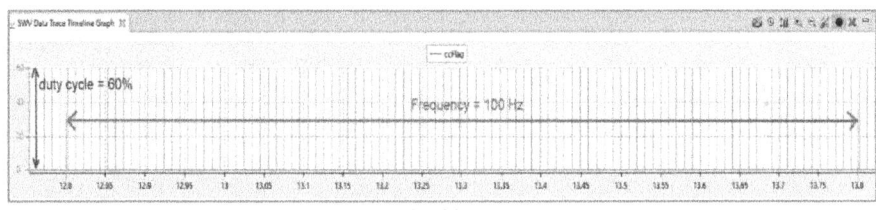

Fig.114

It is seen that our logic analyzer allows us to evaluate two PWM parameters, the base frequency (period) and the duty cycle.

Timer Interrupt Handling: Example 1

Often, we need to handle (enable or disable) a timer interrupt while analyzing code / data flow. This can be done "on the fly" by enabling / disabling the

UIE bit in the TIMx DMA/Interrupt enable register (TIMx_DIER). This example illustrates how to enable / disable Timer 6 (TIM6) global interrupt. To handle this interrupt, we will use register TIM6_DIER. When the interrupt is enabled (bit UIE = 0x1), the code within the Interrupt Handler will toggle the on-board LED (pin **PA5**) every 500 mS. When UIE = 0x0, the interrupt is disabled and the LED stops blinking.

Let's create a new STM32 Project with peripherals configured with their default mode, then activate Timer 6 and enable its interrupt (**Fig.115**).

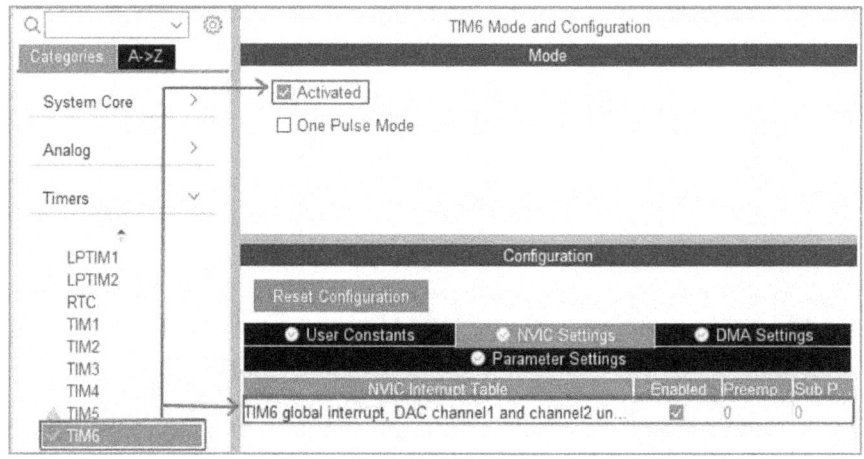

Fig.115

After the Project Wizard has finished its job, we need to modify the source code (**Listing 70**) of the **TIM6_DAC_IRQHandler()** Interrupt Handler (file **stm32l4xx_it.c**).

Listing 70.

void TIM6_DAC_IRQHandler(void)
{
  /* USER CODE BEGIN TIM6_DAC_IRQn 0 */

  /* USER CODE END TIM6_DAC_IRQn 0 */
  HAL_TIM_IRQHandler(&htim6);
  /* USER CODE BEGIN TIM6_DAC_IRQn 1 */

  HAL_GPIO_TogglePin(GPIOA, GPIO_PIN_5);

/* USER CODE END TIM6_DAC_IRQn 1 */
}

Here we added function **HAL_GPIO_TogglePin()** to toggle the on-board LED connected to pin **PA5** configured as output.
Also, we need to set the period of TIM6 overflowing and then enable counting. That is done by modifying the source code (**Listing 71**) of function **MX_TIM6_Init()** (file **main.c**).

Listing 71.

```
static void MX_TIM6_Init(void)
{
. . . . . . .
htim6.Init.Prescaler = 8000;
. . . . . . .
htim6.Init.Period = 10000;
. . . . . . .
HAL_TIM_Base_Start_IT(&htim6);
}
```

In the **main()** function, we must insert a **HAL_Delay()** function into the **while (1)** loop (**Listing 72**).

Listing 72.

```
. . . . . . .
while (1)
  {
  /* USER CODE END WHILE */
  HAL_Delay(10000);
  /* USER CODE BEGIN 3 */
  }
  /* USER CODE END 3 */
. . . . . . .
```

After the project is built without errors, launch the Debugger and open the **SFR** window.
Then we will step through the code until **HAL_Delay(10000)** begins to execute. At this point, we can start / stop blinking the LED by enabling /

disabling the TIM6 interrupt through bit **UIE** in register TIM6_DIER as is illustrated in **Fig.116**.

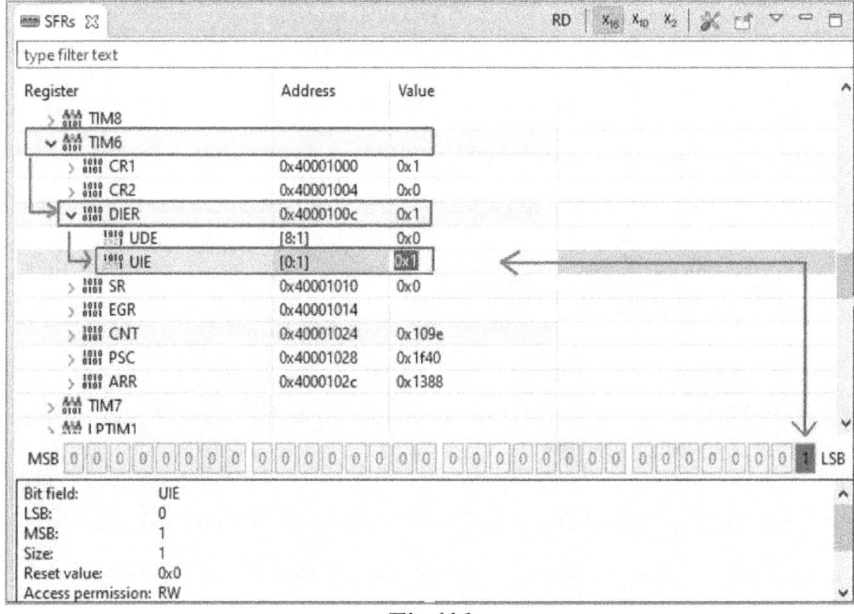

Fig.116

Timer Interrupt Handling: Example 2

We can also enable a timer interrupt by setting the corresponding bit in the interrupt set-enable register (NVIC_ISERx). To disable a timer interrupt, we should set the corresponding bit the interrupt clear-enable registers (NVIC_ICERx).
For example, the following sequence (**Listing 73**) in the **while (1)** loop (file **main.c**) disables / enables TIM6 Interrupt every 10 s.

Listing 73.

```
. . . . . . . .
while (1)
 {
   /* USER CODE END WHILE */
```

```
    HAL_Delay(10000);
    NVIC->ICER[1] |= 0x400000;
    HAL_Delay(10000);
    NVIC->ISER[1] |= 0x400000;
    /* USER CODE BEGIN 3 */
  }
  /* USER CODE END 3 */
```
. . . .

Debugging Direct Digital Synthesis Applications

Direct Digital Synthesis (DDS) is a widely used technique that allows to produce an analog signal (like a sine / triangle wave) by generating a time-varying signal in digital form that can further be converted into a pure analog signal using digital-to-analog conversion. DDS allows to easily configure output frequencies over a broad spectrum with high resolution.

Building a Logic Analyzer: Example 1

In this example, we will see how to:
- program the simple application that can produce the sine waveform;
- build a simple logic analyzer for analyzing a signal;
- handle the frequency of signal in the Debugger.

In this example, we will not output the signal using digital-to-analog conversion.
Let's create a new STM32 Project and allow to configure the peripherals with their default mode. Our application will generate a sine wave signal that will be displayed in the **SWV Data Trace Timeline Graph** window while the application code is debugging. This way we implement a simple logic analyzer for our application.

As a time base reference source, we will use the System Timer whose frequency will determine the frequency of the sine wave signal. To produce the sine wave, we will use a 64-byte Lookup Table (LUT).

Let's modify the source code in the **main.c** and **stm32l4xx_it.c** files. In **stm32f4lxx_it.c**, we need to add a few variables and insert a couple of statements into the **SysTick_Handler()** as is shown in **Listing 74**.

Listing 74.

```
#include "main.h"
#include "stm32l4xx_it.h"

const uint8_t SineTable64[] = {
127, 139, 152, 164, 176, 187, 198, 208, 217, 225, 233, 239, 244, 249, 252, 253,
254, 253, 252, 249, 244, 239, 233, 225, 217, 208, 198, 187, 176, 164, 152, 139,
127, 115, 102, 90, 78, 67, 56, 46, 37, 29, 21, 15, 10, 5, 2, 1,
0, 1, 2, 5, 10, 15, 21, 29, 37, 46, 56, 67, 78, 90, 102, 115
};

volatile uint8_t sineVal;
volatile int i1 = 0;
. . . . . . .

void SysTick_Handler(void)
{
  /* USER CODE BEGIN SysTick_IRQn 0 */

  /* USER CODE END SysTick_IRQn 0 */
  HAL_IncTick();
  /* USER CODE BEGIN SysTick_IRQn 1 */

  if (++i1 > 63) i1 = 0;
  sineVal = SineTable64[i1];

  /* USER CODE END SysTick_IRQn 1 */
}
. . . . . . .
```

In this code, the **SineTable64** array is a Lookup Table (LUT) that contains 64 samples for reproducing a sine wave signal. A particular sample will be stored in the **sineVal** variable.

The sequence

```
if (++i1 > 63) i1 = 0;
sineVal = SineTable64[i1];
```

simply moves a particular sample into **sineVal** and advances the index in array **SineTable64** by 1.

In the **main()** function, we need to add the following statements (shown in bold in **Listing 75**).

Listing 75.

```
#include "main.h"
```
int ticks = 7680; // to produce the sine wave frequency = 120 Hz
. . . .

```
int main(void)
{
```

   HAL_SYSTICK_Config(SystemCoreClock / ticks);

```
   while (1)
   {
      HAL_Delay(20000);
   }
}
```
. . . .

The frequency **SineFreq** of a sinewave signal is calculated using the following formula:

SineFreq = ticks / 64

In our particular case that gives us the following value:

SineFreq = 7680 / 64 = 120 Hz

155

After the project is built without errors, launch the Debugger. Then open the **Serial Wire Viewer** window and enable the **sineVal** variable to be traced (**Fig.117**).

Fig.117

Click **OK** and in the **SWV Data Trace Timeline Graph** window click **Start Trace**. Then step through the instructions until **HAL_Delay()** within the **while(1)** loop begins to execute. At this point, we need to wait some time until data has been collected, then click **"Suspend"** to stop debugging. Then we can adjust the graph to measure the period of signal (≈ 8mS, in our case) as is shown in **Fig.118**.

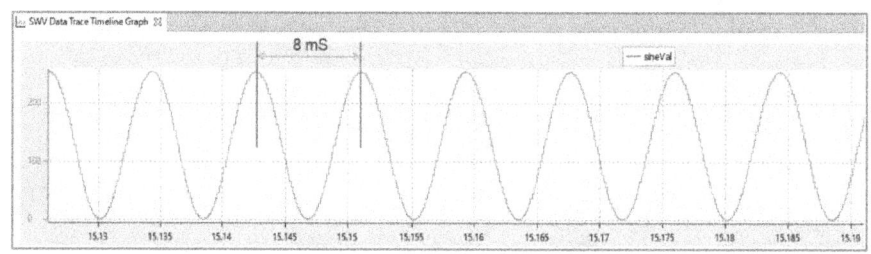

Fig.118

Building a Logic Analyzer: Example 2

This example illustrates how to change the frequency of a sine wave by configuring the frequency of a System Timer. We can use the **main()** code taken from the previous example with minor modifications as is shown in **Listing 76**.

Listing 76.

```
#include "main.h"
const int numSamples = 64; // the size of LUT
int freq = 20; // Initial Sine Wave Freq. = 20 Hz
. . . . . . .

int main(void)
{
while (1)
  {
    HAL_SYSTICK_Config(SystemCoreClock / (freq * numSamples));
    HAL_Delay(200);
  }
}
. . . . . . .
```

In debugging mode, add the **freq** variable to the **Expressions** window and change its values from 60 to 100 (**Fig.119**).

Expression	Type	Value
(x)= freq	int	100
⊕ Add new expression		

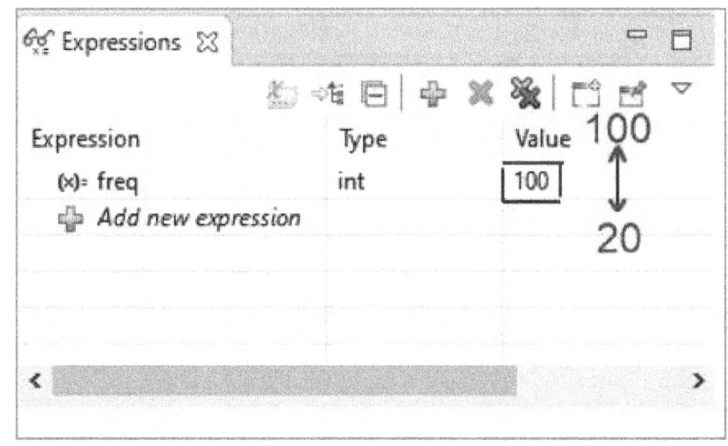

100 ↑↓ 20

Fig.119

Then when we are stepping through the code in the **while (1)** loop, we can observe how the frequency changes from 20 Hz to !00 Hz in the **SWV Data Trace Timeline Graph** window (**Fig.120**).

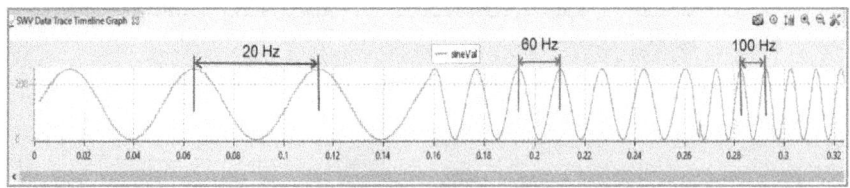

Fig.120

Building a Logic Analyzer: Example 3

In this example, we will build the sine wave generator and output the signal to an analog pin using Digital-to-Analog Converter (DAC). We will also build a logic analyzer to observe the output signal in the
SWV Data Trace Timeline Graph window.
Let's create a new STM32 Project and configure DAC1 output as is illustrated in **Fig.121** - **Fig.122**.

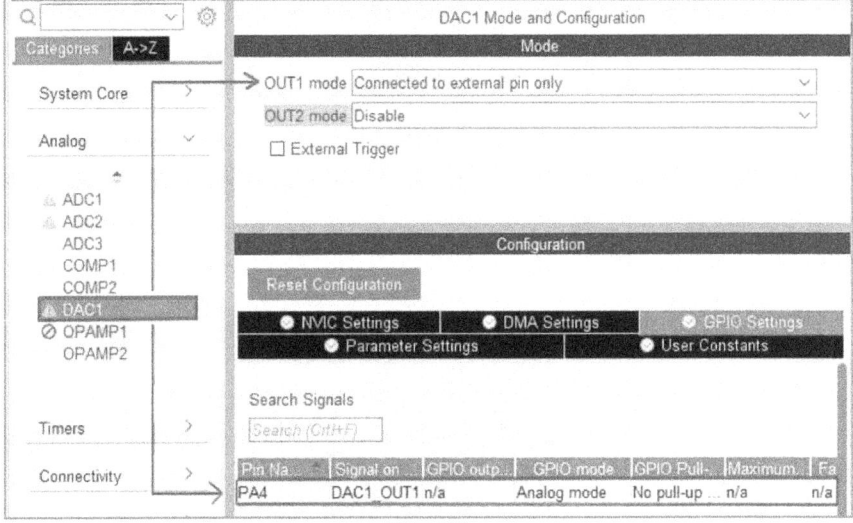

Fig.121

Here we set the OUT1 mode to "**Connected to external pin only**". In this configuration, the output signal will appear on pin **PA4** configured to operate in analog mode. By default, the parameters of D/A conversion are as follows (**Fig.122**). We can leave these unchanged.

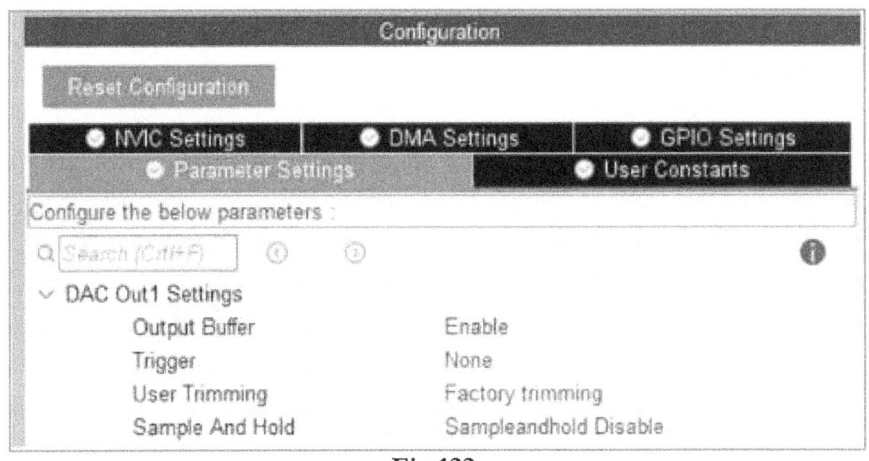

Fig.122

As a time reference source, we will use the basic Timer 6 (TIM6). The configuration window for Timer 6 is shown in **Fig.123**. **Note** that we also need to enable the TIM6 global interrupt.

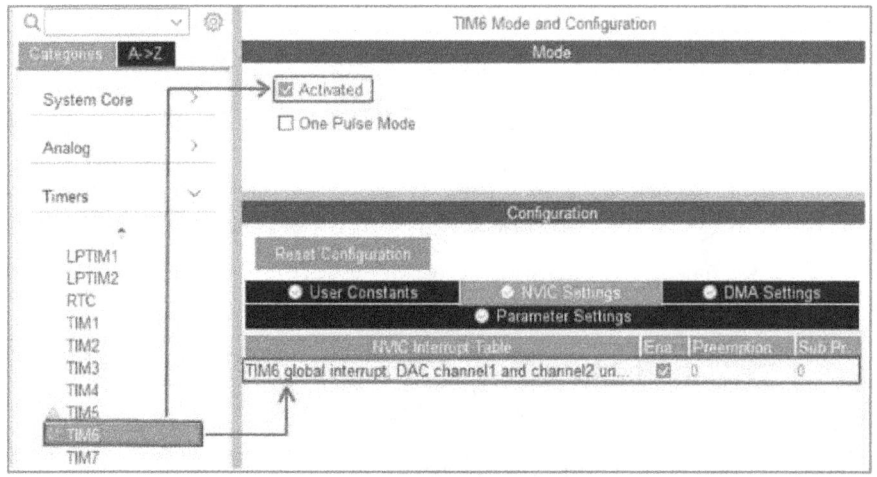

Fig.123

To complete configuring Timer 6, we need to set its overflowing frequency and enable counting. These modifications will be introduced into the source code of function **MX_TIM6_Init()** (file **main.c**) as is shown in **Listing 77**.

Listing 77.

. . . .
htim6.Init.Prescaler = 80;

htim6.Init.Period = 100;
. . . .
HAL_TIM_Base_Start_IT(&htim6);
. . . .

With these parameters, TIM6 overflows every 100 µS (microseconds) that corresponds to the frequency of 10 kHz. This also raises the TIM6 interrupt every 100 µS.

The frequency f_{sine} of a sine wave signal is then calculated through the frequency f_{timer} of timer overflowing as

$f_{sine} = f_{timer} / 64 = 10$ kHz $/ 64 = 156.25$ Hz

Next, we need to modify the source code of the TIM6 Interrupt Handler (function **TIM6_DAC_IRQHandler()** in file **stm2114xx_it.c**). The inserted lines are shown in bold (**Listing 78**).

Listing 78.

```
void TIM6_DAC_IRQHandler(void)
{
  /* USER CODE BEGIN TIM6_DAC_IRQn 0 */

  /* USER CODE END TIM6_DAC_IRQn 0 */
  HAL_TIM_IRQHandler(&htim6);
  //HAL_DAC_IRQHandler(&hdac1);
  /* USER CODE BEGIN TIM6_DAC_IRQn 1 */

  if (++i1 > 63) i1 = 0;
  HAL_DAC_SetValue(&hdac1, DAC_CHANNEL_1,
                   DAC_ALIGN_8B_R, (uint32_t)SineTable64[i1]);
  readDAC = (uint16_t)(HAL_DAC_GetValue(&hdac1,
                   DAC_CHANNEL_1) & 0xfff);

  /* USER CODE END TIM6_DAC_IRQn 1 */
}
```

Here the statement

HAL_DAC_IRQHandler(&hdac1);

is commented because the Interrupt Handler processes only the TIM6 interrupt.

Additionally, we include the following definitions (shown in bold) in file **stm3217xx_it.c** (**Listing 79**).

Listing 79.

```
#include "main.h"
#include "stm32l4xx_it.h"
. . . . . . .
const uint8_t SineTable64[] = {
127, 139, 152, 164, 176, 187, 198, 208, 217, 225, 233, 239, 244, 249, 252, 253,
254, 253, 252, 249, 244, 239, 233, 225, 217, 208, 198, 187, 176, 164, 152, 139,
127, 115, 102, 90, 78, 67, 56, 46, 37, 29, 21, 15, 10, 5, 2, 1,
0, 1, 2, 5, 10, 15, 21, 29, 37, 46, 56, 67, 78, 90, 102, 115
};
volatile int i1 = 0;
volatile uint16_t readDAC;
. . . . . . .
/* External variables --------------------------------------------------------*/
extern DAC_HandleTypeDef hdac1;
extern TIM_HandleTypeDef htim6;
. . . . . . . .
```

In order to start DAC, we place a statement

HAL_DAC_Start(&hdac1, DAC_CHANNEL_1);

at the end of the **MX_DAC1_Init()** function.

In the **main()** function, we place **HAL_Delay()** in the **while (1)** loop of the **main()** function (**Listing 80**).

Listing 80.

```
. . . . . . .
while (1)
  {
   /* USER CODE END WHILE */
   HAL_Delay(10000);
   /* USER CODE BEGIN 3 */
  }
. . . . . . .
```

After the project is built without errors, we can launch the Debugger and examine the data (variable **readDAC**) that appears in the **SWV Data Trace Timeline Graph** window (**Fig.124**).

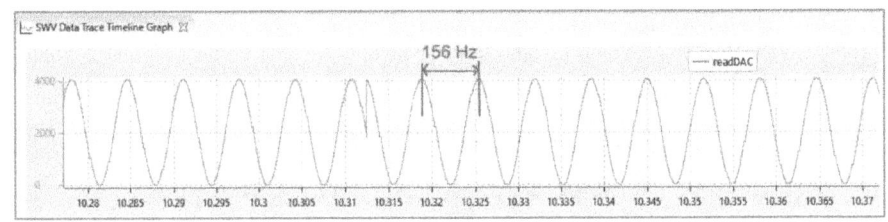

Fig.124

Building a Logic Analyzer: Example 4

It easily to create an application that produces wave forms other than sine wave. This may be done by introducing the LUT designed for specific signal. This example illustrates how to build a logic analyzer for a DDS application producing a triangle signal. To do that, we will take the code from the previous example and modify it.
First, we define the LUT for triangle waveform in file **stm32l4xx_it.c**:

const uint8_t TriangleTable63[] = {
0, 1, 2, 3, 4, 5, 6, 7, 8, 9, 10, 11, 12, 13, 14, 15,
16, 17, 18, 19, 20, 21, 22, 23, 24, 25, 26, 27, 28, 29, 30, 31,
30, 29, 28, 27, 26, 25, 24, 23, 22, 21, 20, 19, 18, 17, 16, 15,
14, 13, 12, 11, 10, 9, 8, 7, 6, 5, 4, 3, 2, 1, 0
};

Second, we change the corresponding parameter in function **HAL_DAC_SetValue()** and condition in the **if()** statement within the **TIM6_DAC_IRQHandler()** Interrupt Handler (file **stm32l4xx_it.c**).

The source code of **TIM6_DAC_IRQHandler()** will then look like the following (**Listing 81**).

Listing 81.

void TIM6_DAC_IRQHandler(void)
{
  /* USER CODE BEGIN TIM6_DAC_IRQn 0 */

```
/* USER CODE END TIM6_DAC_IRQn 0 */
HAL_TIM_IRQHandler(&htim6);
//HAL_DAC_IRQHandler(&hdac1);
/* USER CODE BEGIN TIM6_DAC_IRQn 1 */

if (++i1 > 62) i1 = 0;
HAL_DAC_SetValue(&hdac1, DAC_CHANNEL_1,
        DAC_ALIGN_8B_R,
        (uint32_t)TriangleTable63[i1]);
readDAC = (uint16_t)(HAL_DAC_GetValue(&hdac1,
        DAC_CHANNEL_1) & 0xfff);

/* USER CODE END TIM6_DAC_IRQn 1 */
}
```

When we are done, build the project and launch the Debugger. Then we can observe the triangle signal (variable **readDAC**) in the **SWV Data Trace Timeline Graph** window (**Fig.125**).

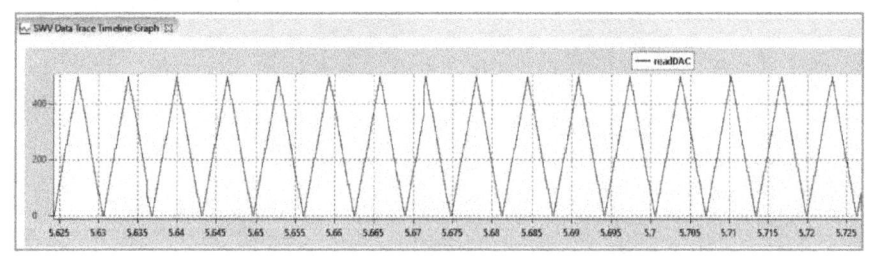

Fig.125

Measuring and Tracing Analog Signals

This section is dedicated to programming and debugging the applications that process low-frequency analog signals using Analog-to-Digital Converters (ADCs). Here we will build the simple logic analyzers for viewing and examining signals from ADC.

In STM32 microcontrollers, analog-to-digital conversion can be implemented in various ways. We will use the simplest way where ADC operates in polling mode which includes 4 steps:

1. Starting the ADC peripheral using the **HAL_ADC_Start()** function;

2. Waiting for end of conversion using the **HAL_ADC_PollForConversion()** function;
3. Reading the ADC converted values using the **HAL_ADC_GetValue()** function;
4. Stopping the ADC peripheral using the **HAL_ADC_Stop()** function.

The above sequence can be performed periodically within the Interrupt Handler of a timer and a result can be output to the **SWV Data Trace Timeline Graph** window. Thus, we get the simplest digital scope for measuring analog signals. Of course, we can't provide the exact measurement for fast signals of a few ten kHz, but for a relatively sow signals this works quite well.

Example 1

In this example, we will build a digital scope based upon using a System Timer. For my NUCLEO-L476RG board, the system clock SYSCLK is equal to 80 MHz. Recall that this frequency is divided by 8 (=10 MHz) to feed the System Timer with the configurable output frequency (by default, 1000 Hz (Period = 1mS).
We will change this output frequency so that to process analog signals of a few hundred Hz without distortion.
Let's create a new STM32 Project and select the Analog-to-Digital converter ADC1. To capture input data, choose channel **IN5** (**Fig.126**).

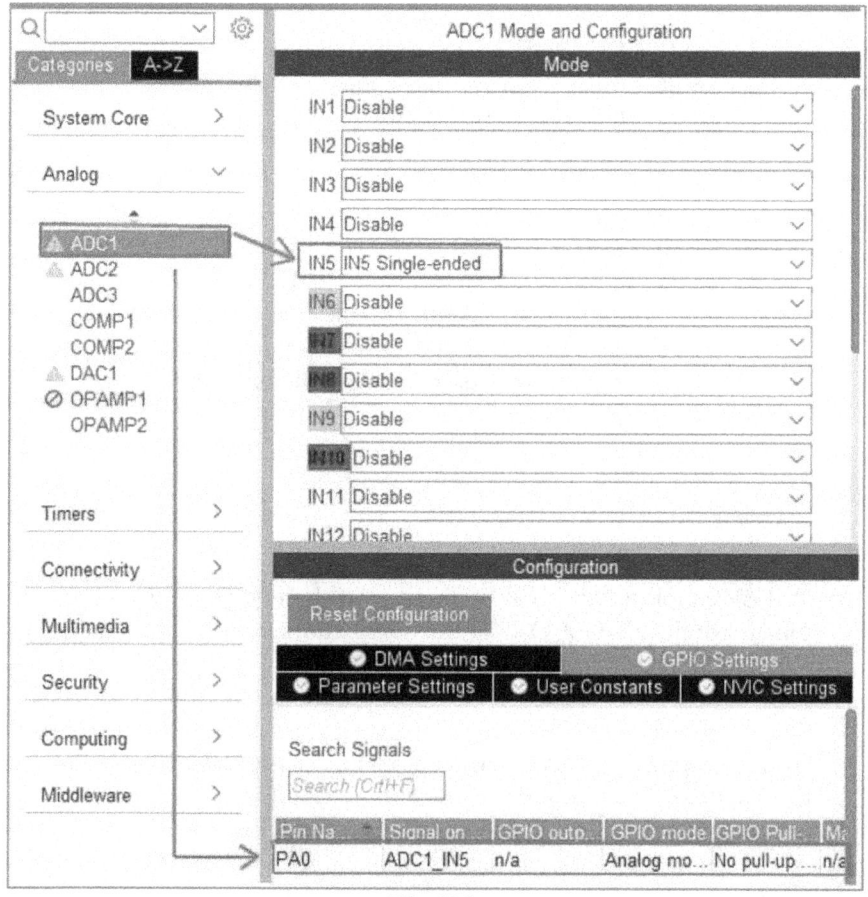

Fig.126

Channel **IN5** will be configured to operate in single-ended mode. We also need to set a few parameters on the **Configuration** page (**Fig.127**).

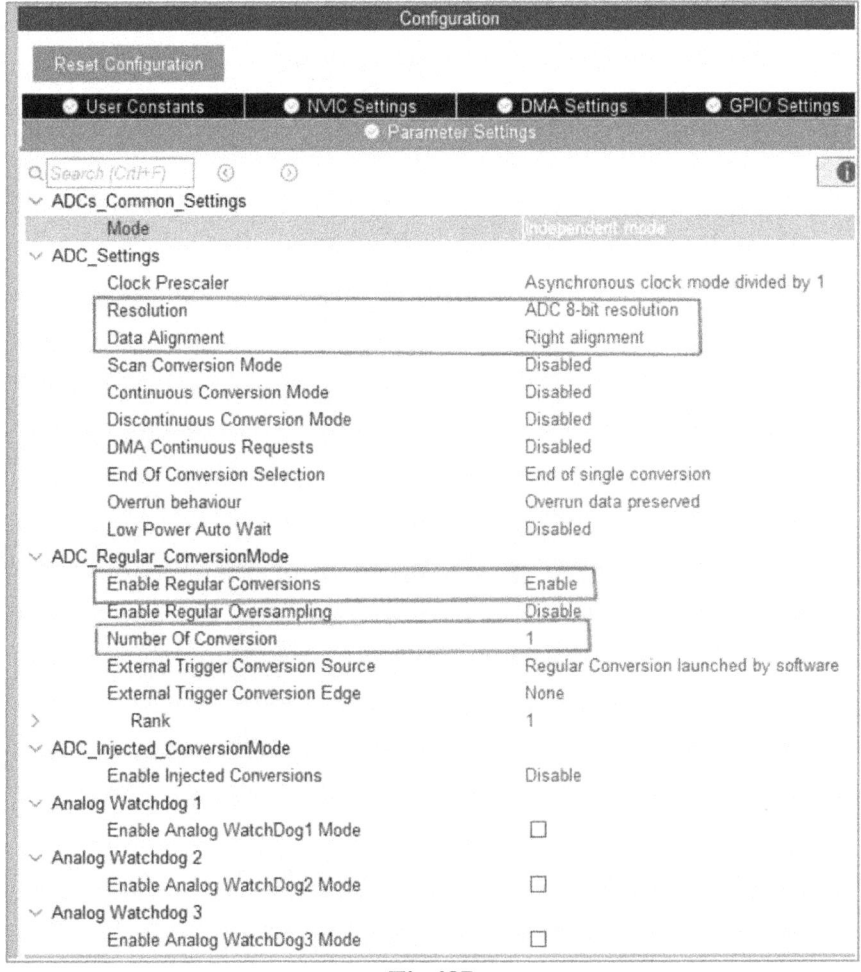

Fig.127

In this particular case, we select 8-bit resolution with right alignment. Also, parameter **Enable Regular Conversions** must be enabled. The **Number Of Conversions** parameter must be set to 1.
When we are done, generate (update) the code.

At the next step, we will modify the source code of the **main()** function (**Listing 82**). The inserted lines are shown in bold.

Listing 82.

```
. . . . . . .
int main(void)
{

   . . . . . . .

   HAL_SYSTICK_Config(SystemCoreClock / 10000);
   while (1)
   {
     HAL_Delay(10000);
   }
}
   . . . . . . .
```

The period of System Timer is set $1/10000 = 0.1\text{mS} = 100\ \mu\text{S}$ - that is enough to process the single conversion of a low-frequency analog signal. As usual, we place the **HAL_Delay()** function within the **while(1)** loop.

Next, we modify the source code of **SysTick_Handler()** (file **stm32l4xx_it.c**). The inserted statements are shown in bold (**Listing 83**).

Listing 83.

```
void SysTick_Handler(void)
{
  /* USER CODE BEGIN SysTick_IRQn 0 */

  /* USER CODE END SysTick_IRQn 0 */
  HAL_IncTick();

  /* USER CODE BEGIN SysTick_IRQn 1 */

  HAL_ADC_Start(&hadc1);
  HAL_ADC_PollForConversion(&hadc1, 10);
  Dn = (uint8_t)HAL_ADC_GetValue(&hadc1);
  HAL_ADC_Stop(&hadc1);

  /* USER CODE END SysTick_IRQn 1 */
}
```

Also, we add a few definitions at the beginning of the **stm32l4xx_it.c** file (shown in bold in **Listing 84**).

Listing 84.

#include "main.h"
#include "stm32l4xx_it.h"

extern ADC_HandleTypeDef hadc1;
volatile uint8_t Dn;
. . . .

When we are done, build the project and launch the Debugger. Here we open the **SWV Data Trace Timeline Graph** window and add variable **Dn** to the configuration page (**Fig.128**).

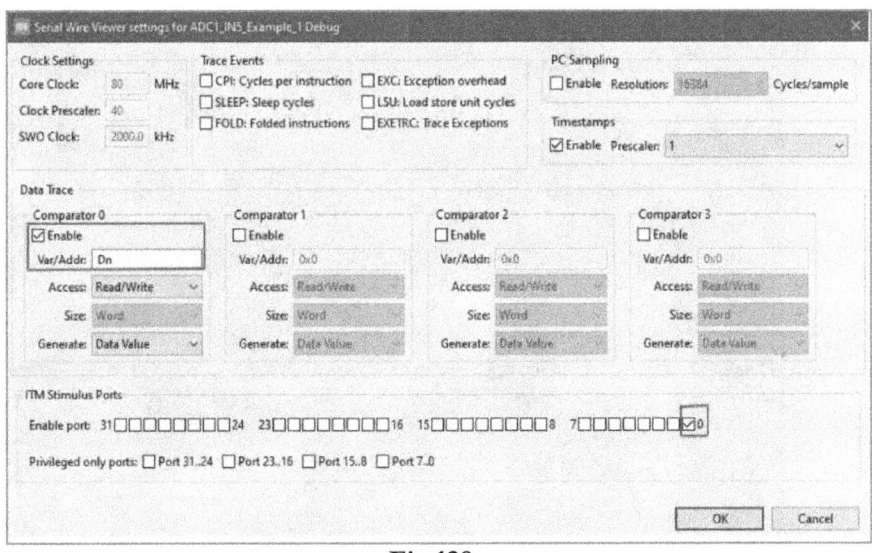

Fig.128

While executing the **HAL_Delay()** in a **while(1)** loop, the analog signal is being output in the timeline graph window (**Fig.129**).

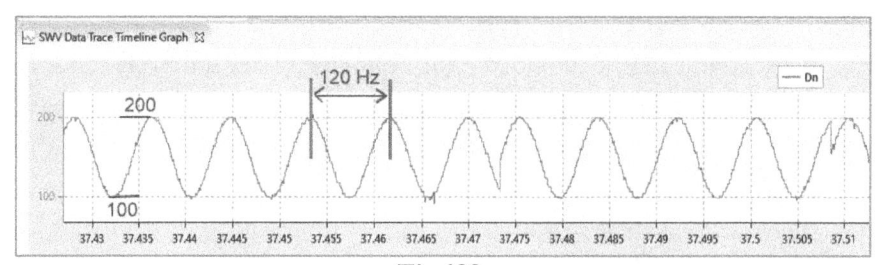

Fig.129

To test the application, I used the sine wave with a frequency of 120 Hz and magnitude of 1.2V. This signal was also measured using a digital USB scope (**Fig.130**).

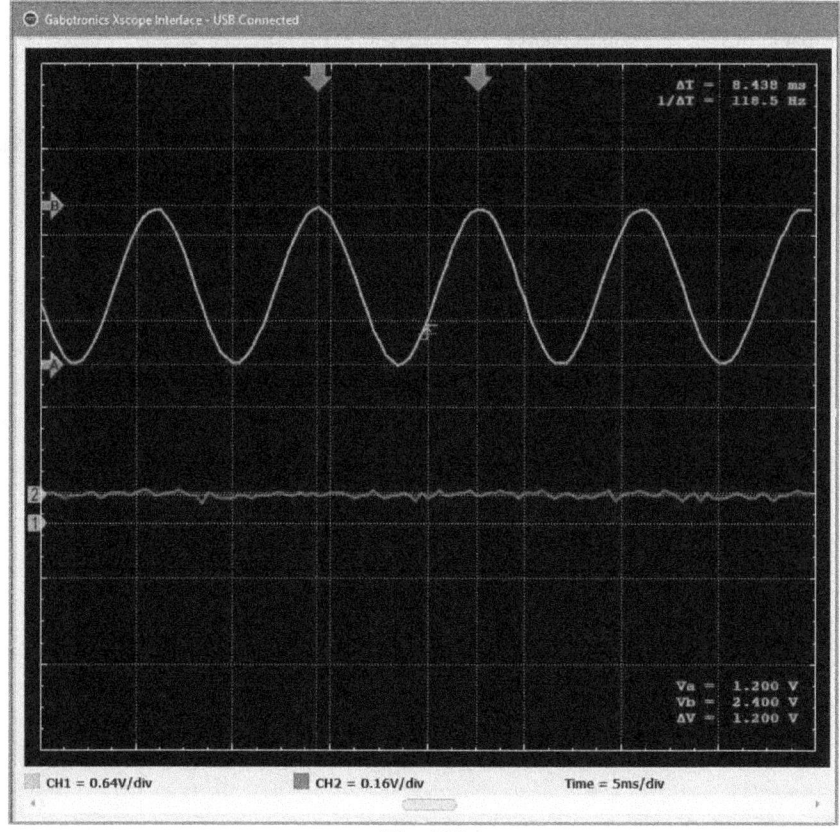

Fig.130

Example 2

To observe and examine analog signals, we can build a digital scope that uses some STM32 basic timer. In this example, we use the basic Timer 6 (TIM6) that will be used as generic timers for time base generation.
Let's create a new STM32 Project with default settings for peripherals devices. Then activate Timer 6 and enable its interrupt as is shown in **Fig.131**.

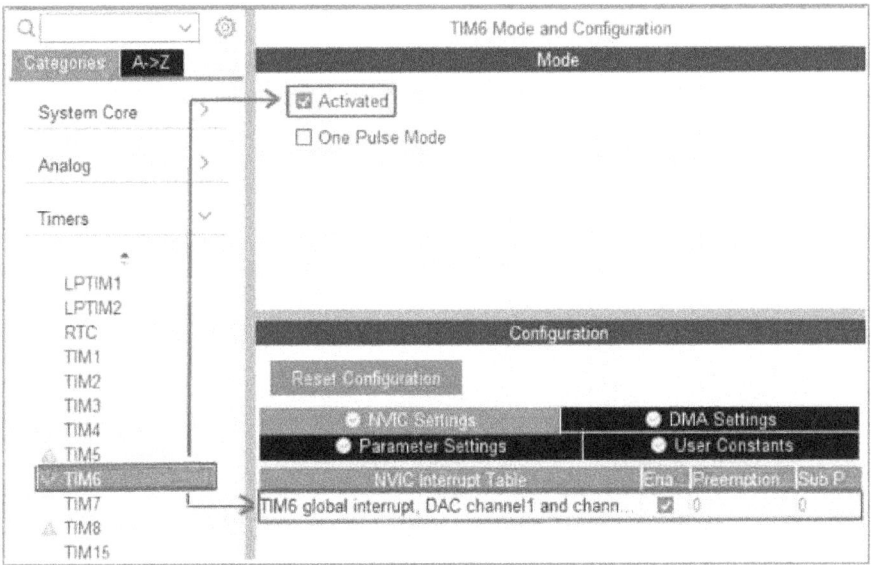

Fig.131

To process analog signals, we will use channel **IN5** of ADC1 whose configuration was described in detail in the previous example.
After generating the code, we need to introduce some changes into files **main.c** and **stm32l4xx_it.c**.

To complete configuring TIM6, we need to set the frequency of overflowing and enable counting. These modifications will be introduced into the source code of function **MX_TIM6_Init()** (file **main.c**) as is shown in **Listing 85**.

Listing 85.

. . . .

htim6.Init.Prescaler = 80;

htim6.Init.Period = 100;

. . . .

HAL_TIM_Base_Start_IT(&htim6);

. . . .

With these parameters, the timer interrupt will be activated every 100 μS (microseconds) that corresponds to the frequency of 10 kHz.

Next, we need to modify the source code of the TIM6 Interrupt Handler (function **TIM6_DAC_IRQHandler()** in file **stm2114xx_it.c**). The inserted lines are shown in bold (**Listing 86**).

Listing 86.

void TIM6_DAC_IRQHandler(void)
{
  /* USER CODE BEGIN TIM6_DAC_IRQn 0 */

  /* USER CODE END TIM6_DAC_IRQn 0 */
  HAL_TIM_IRQHandler(&htim6);
  /* USER CODE BEGIN TIM6_DAC_IRQn 1 */

  HAL_ADC_Start(&hadc1);
  HAL_ADC_PollForConversion(&hadc1, 10);
  Dn = (uint8_t)HAL_ADC_GetValue(&hadc1);
  HAL_ADC_Stop(&hadc1);

  /* USER CODE END TIM6_DAC_IRQn 1 */
}

Also, we add the following definitions (shown in bold) at the beginning of file **stm32l7xx_it.c** (**Listing 87**).

Listing 87.

#include "main.h"
#include "stm32l4xx_it.h"

. . . .

extern ADC_HandleTypeDef hadc1;
volatile uint8_t Dn;

. . . .

Finally, we place a **HAL_Delay()** in the **while (1)** loop (file **main.c**, **Listing 88**).

Listing 88.

```
. . . . . . .
while (1)
  {
  /* USER CODE END WHILE */
  HAL_Delay(10000);
  /* USER CODE BEGIN 3 */
  }
. . . . . . .
```

After building the project, we can launch the Debugger and examine the data that appears in the **SWV Data Trace Timeline Graph** window.

Index

Analog-to-Digital Converters, 164
BKPT instruction, 77
boundary address, 101
breakpoint, 76
clocking, 102
Command Shell Console, 72
Core Clock, 15
Debugger, 13
Digital-to-Analog conversion, 153
Direct Digital Synthesis, 153
Disassembly window, 30
exception, 78
Exception Handler, 78
Expressions window, 16
external interrupt, 121
FPU, 78
GPIO, 108
Instrumentation Trace Macrocell, 58
interrupts, 106
ITM port, 58

Live Expressions window, 16
logic analyzer, 140
Memory Browser, 20
Memory window, 20
memory-mapped registers, 100
Monitors page, 23
NVIC, 78
peripherals, 98
pin alternate functions, 108
PWM, 134
Registers window, 25
Serial Wire Viewer, 116
SFR window, 116
supervisor call, 89
SVC, 89
SWD interface, 58
SYSCLK, 15
Timeline Graph, 114
Timer, 133
USB-UART interface, 67

CPSIA information can be obtained
at www.ICGtesting.com
Printed in the USA
LVHW091335270521
688682LV00003B/162